TIME WORTH $PENDING

The Top 10 Talks to Have with Your Teenager About Money

PATRICIA SAUNDERS GARFIELD

ALYSON AMY EDGE

To the students and parents of the Academy of Finance
at Burbank High School,
you inspired us to write this book and inspire us to teach.

Acknowledgements

We are indebted to many people whose help has made this book possible:

First of all, we thank the community of Burbank High School whose students, parents, faculty, administration and staff educated us and consistently encouraged us along the way.

Thank you to our multi-talented editor, Susan Ruffins, who guided us and cheered us on throughout the process. You are so much more than a brilliant editor; we are truly grateful to you.

For loving us always and teaching us about many things, including personal finance, we thank our parents: Elizabeth and Richard Saunders, Marlee and Keith Edge.

A very special thank you to our own families who put up with the disruption of this project and remained enthusiastic throughout. We thank you George, Taylor and Peter Garfield, and Ismael and Jacob Lopez.

To Jonelle Pickett, our very creative graphic artist, who made black and white text and charts come to life and tell a story in a way our words alone never could. Many thanks.

For sharing their stories, providing support, technical advice, and creative ideas we thank:

John Adamson, Kelly Arthur, Gary Arzumanyan, Frank Baldinelli, Vida Barone, Laura and Tom Bernhardt, Robert Bjorklund, Isaac Blackburn, Sue Boegh, Allyson Burakoff, Ben Carey, Marci Carisch, Monika Chamichyan, Mindy Clark, Tom Conforti, Erica Cooper, Amy Danforth, Troy DeChellis, Paula Denney, Mauro Diaz, Todd Doney, Lindi Dreibelbis Arthur, Tracey and Gery English, David Escobar, Teri Forlizzi, Bill Gallimore, Youlen Ghazalian, Terri, Chuck and John Gilbert, Tom Gilligan, Janna and Craig Gosselin, Brady Griffin, Doug Grimshaw, Mary and Ashot Hareyan, Joe Hefner, Mary Hogen, Tara Karamians, Susan Karsian, Erik Kimoto, Debbie and Matt Kukta, Sarkis Kulakchyan, Renee LaBran-Boyd, Andy Levinson, Manolo Lopez, Barb Maduell, Erin Mann, Lance Markowitz, Zara Matevosyan, Bruno Maynez, Francie McCarthy, Suzanne McClure, Paul McNiff, Mark Melacaro, Valente Montes, Luther Moore, April Moreno, Carrie O'Keefe, Bruce Osgood, Sousanna Pogosyan, Leonardo Tito Proano, Mandy and Sunder Ramani, Andrea Reyes, Ray Reynolds, Tony Richman, Shelley Rizzotti, Erika Rochana, KC Rondinella, Anne Schulze, Bill Sparks, Mark Sprague, Jackie Stein, Agavni Tabakian, Elyce Talavera, Michelle, Judy, and Dave Van Wyk, Andrea Walker, and Hani Youssef.

And thank you to the following organizations that have supported our students and the Academy of Finance program at Burbank High School over many years:

Burbank City Federal Credit Union
Burbank Unified School District
The City of Burbank, Youth Services
Junior Achievement of Southern California
Los Angeles County Regional Occupational Program
The National Academy Foundation
Woodbury University

Table of Contents

Section I

Section II

Section III

Introduction & Welcome

Over dinner at a local Indian restaurant, a friend told us a funny story. Her nephew had started his sophomore year as a math major at Carnegie Mellon University. He had always been something of a math 'whiz', even as a young boy, and in high school had received a Governor's Award as one of the five top math students in the state. His parents were quite proud when he was admitted to CMU's math program, a tough and well regarded place where they knew he would get a true mental workout. In recognition of his advanced math abilities, he was selected as a teaching assistant in his second year. The job came with a student stipend of $500 a semester. He knew he wanted to replace his computer in the spring, so a stipend would really help.

Between school, work and his social life, he was pretty busy and didn't always have the chance to get to the bank. Instead he would run to the campus cash machine, even though he knew the bank charged him a small fee with each withdrawal. He also didn't keep track of his account balance, but he figured that since he was able to withdraw funds regularly, his balance was still positive. Toward the end of the semester he finally got a moment to catch up with a stack of mail which had been slowly accumulating off to one side of his desk. Letter after letter was from the bank. Each time he opened one, a thin slip of paper reported that he had withdrawn excess funds and was charged

a fee. In total he had something like twenty overdraft notices. Now in a cold sweat, he headed to the bank and spoke with a teller who reconciled his account. Overall he had depleted his checking account and the overdraft coverage of his savings account. There were only a few dollars left in his savings account when there should have been hundreds. The difference? The bank had deducted about $500 in overdraft charges and fees. His semester stipend? It went straight to pay the bank.

"How could such a smart kid be such an idiot?" our friend wondered. Well, we can confidently report that he isn't the only one. This sort of scenario is not uncommon with young people. The root of the problem is that most teens don't have any financial education and make mistakes…sometimes over and over again. Quite honestly, this isn't just a problem among young people. Financial ignorance is everywhere. So, do financially savvy teens have a leg up on the peers? Absolutely.

That's where we try to help. Our new book, *Time Worth Spending* provides a roadmap for parents and teenagers to learn about money together – how to earn it, save it, spend it, invest it and give it away. Our top ten financial lessons teach teens the basics of money management and prepare them for a lifetime of financial decision making which will enrich their lives and help them take that crucial step toward financial independence.

The financial landscape in the U.S. grows more complex each year, yet students are less informed about basic finances than ever. Among U.S. young adults, financial ignorance is the norm. A 2009 Financial Literacy Survey of adults, conducted on behalf of the National Foundation For Credit Counseling, Inc., revealed that 41% of U.S. adults, more than 90 million people, gave themselves a grade of C, D, or F on their knowledge of personal finance. They also worried about their children's lack of financial savvy. According to a 2008 survey by the Hartford Financial Services Group, Inc., 55% of parents with children aged 16-24 voiced concern about their children's ability to become financially independent without parental assistance. Nearly 72% of the parents surveyed acknowledged that they are their children's primary source of personal finance education, yet 44% admit to needing guidance on how to best teach their children the skills necessary to become financially responsible.

The pressure on teens to spend money is enormous. According to a report by Mintel – a leader of competitive media, product and consumer intelligence – direct teen spending topped $175 billion in 2006. In addition, parents buying for teens spent an additional $100 billion. There is a lot of marketing savvy at work to separate teens from their (and let's face it, your) money. It's time to recognize that learning how to spend, save and invest money is crucial for young people. The earlier they can put sound financial practices to work in their lives, the better prepared they'll be to handle the inevitable ups and downs of economic life. They'll also be better prepared to participate in the financial life of their own communities and feel greater control over their own financial destiny.

We recognize that we are aiming high. Yet for the past 25 years we've helped young adults learn about the best ways to handle money. As credentialed educators with expertise in finance and investing, we understand the issues, phobias and confusion surrounding money management. This spurred us to write *Time Worth Spending* and to partner with parents in spreading our message of financial literacy. We've structured our book to include hands-on activities that parents and teens do together like developing a budget and paying the bills. This creates an authentic shared learning experience and gives parents the opportunity to speak frankly with their kids about money.

Time Worth Spending is targeted at two audiences. The first audience is parents with children preparing to "leave the nest" and head off to college. The second audience is parents whose children "hang around the nest" while working and/or commuting to college. No matter which audience you belong to, the concepts and activities in *Time Worth Spending* are ones that all teenagers should understand and practice before they are expected to be responsible with their own earnings.

Money is a real world issue – something that teens focus little on, in part because so many of us parents have a hard time broaching the topic of household finances. It's time for that aspect of American prudishness to disappear. We believe that teens should not only be empowered to make financial-related decisions once they leave home, but be able to start making better financial choices almost immediately. Whenever either of us talks about what we teach — whether with family, friends, acquaintances, or strangers — we are always met with a similar response. It goes something like this: "I wish they had those classes at my kid's school. Heck, I need those classes. Our country needs those classes."

But before you start, we have a word of advice: If your teenager is like the ones we teach, they aren't jumping at the chance to save money or learn about taxes. Life right now has plenty of other challenges. We know that. So the stories and activities we've designed are meant to engage the teenager and hopefully lead to a few "Aha!" moments. They are also designed to meet both parent and teen wherever you are in your personal financial education. Whether your teen becomes a successful hedge fund manager or remains someone who shies away from the 'F-word' (finance), or somewhere in between, the activities in *Time Worth Spending* teach simple yet fundamental lessons that will last a lifetime.

Just remember:

We all have to use money to survive — our entire lives! Personal finance is a topic we cannot afford to skip over with our children.

How to Use This Book

Time Worth Spending is organized into ten Chapters, with three major areas of emphasis:

1. Mastering basic banking and money etiquette

2. Planning and paying for college and technical school

3. Starting life out on solid financial footing

Section I (Chapters One, Two and Three) covers basic financial life lessons that every teen needs to master. Chapter One encourages teens to open checking and savings accounts, familiarize themselves with how bank accounts work, use an ATM card and keep track of income and expenses. In Chapter Two, teens learn basic money etiquette like how to calculate a tip, how to split a bill with friends, the best ways to be charitable with time and money and how to evaluate volunteer organizations. Chapter Three tackles the very real, very scary truths of credit cards – the benefits, the pitfalls, and the real cost of accumulating credit card debit.

Section II of this book (Chapters Four, Five and Six) helps you and your teen together build a decision map to navigate life after high school. It starts with Chapter Four, *Where's Your Passion?* In this chapter teens begin to define their career interests and research the future education they'll need in order to reach their professional goals. They'll also look at the big picture, i.e. how much is their chosen career likely to pay once their education and credentials are acquired. From there, Chapter Five prompts teens to begin collecting information about colleges. What are the schools that teens can apply to that can meet their professional goals and what will those schools cost for an education? Now the big question: How to pay for it all? You and your teen will spend time learning about all the different sources of money to help pay for school and spend time considering debt financing and what it really will take to pay it all back. Chapter Six helps familiarize your teen with the notion of 'budgeting' both now as a high school student and through college or technical school. Together you will build a realistic budget for Year 1 of college/technical school and determine the cost and payment sources for all years

of school combined.   This chapter also contains lots of 'snapshots' – different budgets of students working through all the costs of their post high school educations.   To help make it all crystal clear, we've included a final chart that will hold your most critical college or technical decision data.   By the end of this section, you and your teen should have a working plan to help you zero in on the right school for the right education at the right price.

Section III (Chapters Seven, Eight, Nine and Ten) touches on a variety of financial topics that will impact your teen's life in the near future.   This includes preparing for job interviews and the workplace, understanding the financial trade-offs between buying and leasing a car, the reality of taxes and how it impacts income and lifestyle post college, and why saving and investing money is the best way for young people to accumulate wealth over time.   Topics in this section can be tackled in the order that best suits you and your teen.

Time Worth Spending was intentionally designed as an activity based workbook to help your teenager recognize and understand life's upcoming financial challenges and to create an action plan to get you both through it in good financial health.

Section 1

Chapter 1
MISSION CRITICAL: Banking Fundamentals

"The art is not in making money, but in keeping it."

- Proverb

MISSION CRITICAL:
Banking
Fundamentals

GOAL: To have teens open bank accounts and begin managing their personal finances independently.

In the 1600s, it was common in England for money to be stored in kitchen pots. Those pots were made from a type of clay called "pygg". By the 1700s, the word "pygg" had changed to "pig" and potters began to craft the jars into the shape of a pig. No surprise that over time the jar became known as the "piggy bank."

Most of us grew up with a piggy bank, a place we could keep our loose change. If we fiddled hard enough with the lock on the bottom, we could open the bank and take out money when we heard the ice cream truck heading around the corner. Our children also received piggy banks and had fun dropping coins into the slot. Generation to generation, most children have learned two lessons from their piggy banks – it's important to save money and it's important to keep it in a safe place. In this chapter we'll take that lesson right to the bank and help your teen start managing their funds.

First things first. Having a relationship with a commercial bank or credit union is absolutely essential for your teenager. If your teen doesn't already have a savings account, now is the time to make it happen. In our experience, it's actually more likely that a teen has a savings account where (hopefully) a portion of his or her earnings from odd jobs, summer work, and birthday money has been stashed. That's good. But we recommend that teenagers also open a checking account. Not only because of the additional services it provides, but because the activity of checking accounts gives teens real life experience in managing the inflow and outflow of funds.   Remember, your teen is the one opening banking accounts, not you. You'll need to be there, of course, but let your son or daughter become the true 'owner' of the accounts.

Now before you go to the bank, discuss the "why, where and how" with your teen:

Why Do You Need a Savings Account?

The best reason to have a savings account is to set money aside on a regular basis to provide for future needs. Sometimes these needs are expected – social events such as prom and birthdays – and sometimes they're unexpected – emergencies such as a tire blow out or lost a cell phone. Saving is also an essential step to investing, but let's save that 'talk' with your teenager for Chapter 10, *A Little Now, A Latte Later: Saving and Investing For Your Future.* Finally, don't forget to mention that a bank is much more secure than a piggy bank and can provide your teen with on-time accounting to help keep track of all account transactions.

Where Should the Account Be Located?

Talk about where the best place to have an account. Is it where you bank? Does your teen's school offer a branch of a local credit union right on campus? Keep in mind that you are helping your teen establish their financial habits, including the everyday act of going to the bank. If your bank is across town or you rely on direct deposit and online banking, let your teen choose someplace more convenient for him or her.

How to Begin Saving

Back to our piggy bank. Most children get them when they are young but have outgrown them by their teenage years. Instead, find a cool savings jar for your teen to start saving coins on a daily basis. One we love is a battery operated coin jar that displays the amount inside. It's a great tool to help you reach a certain savings goal.

Your teen should get into the routine of emptying their pockets, backpack, and/or purse of loose change and deposit these coins into the savings jar daily. In fact, do it together and drop your loose change in there too. At the end of a month, take the coins to the bank and deposit them into their savings account. Talk with your teen about how easy it is for change to add up and help their savings accounts to grow!

Continue with this routine all year and make time once a month for a deposit into the savings account. This loose change will add up, and it will make a difference.

Checking Accounts & Their Advantages

We recommend that all teenagers open a checking account at the same bank or credit union where they have a savings account.

A checking account offers several advantages:

- Debit cards and checks are often safer and more convenient than cash.

- It provides a convenient way to pay bills.

- A checking account has a built-in record keeping system that can help your teenager track transactions.

DOLLARS & $ENSE

Carlos looked confused and a little ticked off after the teacher explained the assignment. How was he supposed to collect loose change – a meaningful amount – and then deposit it into a savings account? He never had loose change; his mother didn't give him spending money and he didn't have any means of earning money. And a savings account? He wasn't even sure what that was exactly. And why would he need to save anyway? For what? His mother bought him things, like clothes and school supplies, when he needed them.

After class, Carlos hesitantly approached the teacher. "I can't do the assignment. I don't ever have loose change and I don't have a savings account. This seems kinda dumb anyway."

Refraining from strangling the boy for calling the assignment "dumb", the teacher offered, "In the not so distant future, you will need to be in charge of your own money and this is the first step in learning how to do that. You have a good, creative brain in that head of yours, so why don't you think about a way to get some change and in the meantime ask your mother to let you open a savings account."

A week or so later, Carlos came to the teacher at the beginning of class, very excited. "I want to let you know that I've started collecting some change by recycling cans and bottles. Yesterday I got about $8.00. And I put that in an old Superman pencil box I've had since I was little. That's going to be my 'savings jar'."

The teacher smiled, and praised Carlos for such a creative and worthy effort. Then she asked about the savings account. Carlos smiled back and said, "Oh yeah, my mom said OK and I have one now at Wells Fargo."

Throughout the year, the students were required to make periodic deposits into their savings account using the money collected in their 'savings jars'. By the end of the year Carlos had collected and saved about $60. Carlos admitted, "I would have never thought that recycling cans and bottles would earn me that much. And it wasn't even hard – it was actually kinda fun."

- Your teen will have access to other services such as online banking, ATMs and automatic deposit.

Teens need to familiarize themselves with online banking and debit cards. Yes, they've seen you use these services for years, but there is a certain "whoa" moment when your teenager swipes their debit card for the first time. It suddenly seems a little more complicated than they thought. Some of their day-to-day banking needs will take place in front of an ATM so it is critical that they be absolutely comfortable with this process too. From there it is a hop, skip and jump before they move onto **online banking** services that will allow them to pay bills or transfer funds from a computer or cell phone.

We also recommend that teens learn to write checks, however outdated they may find that idea. Even in today's highly automated and interconnected banking world, there are still certain situations where you can't pay with cash or a credit card.

Now it's time to take some action:

Step #1: Practice Makes Perfect
Before setting up bank accounts, have your teenager practice managing money.
Something that we will all do the rest of our lives once we start is . . . pay the bills! The best way for your teen to learn how to pay the bills is to participate with you. Don't be afraid to get them involved. Remember, it can be a learning experience for both of you. Next time you need to pay the bills, have your teen sit right next to you. First, start with opening all of the envelopes and talking about each statement.

Ask them to look over each bill and find:
- What's the bill for?
- The due date
- The bill total
- The minimum amount due
- Any past due amounts
- Any late fees
- Any interest or finance charges
- Where is it to be sent, if mailed?

For many it will be the first time they have ever noticed how much the family pays for the cable bill or even for the basic utilities. Many teens are shocked to see the high costs of basic family expenses. That's a real world wake up call!

Step #2: Practice Check Writing
Teach your teen how to write a check using the blank forms on page 8. We suggest using a pencil each time, so you can erase and refresh as many times as needed. Have them practice filling out a check a few times until you feel they understand. Once you feel they are ready, have them slowly write a check for the utility bill. Have them write it out in pencil so you know they are going to write it correctly before they get started.

Now it's time to write the first real check. Watch over them as they fill in the date, the payee, the dollar amount and the number in long form. Discuss if there is anything you would like to write in the memo line. You sign the check.

Be sure to take time to show your teen how to complete the check register and keep the account balance up to date. Discuss how important it is to write in the check register and always know the balance in your checking account.

MY SAMPLE CHECK   20

Pay to the order of: $

                                                          Dollars

Memo:

MY SAMPLE CHECK   20

Pay to the order of: $

                                                          Dollars

Memo:

MY SAMPLE CHECK   20

Pay to the order of: $

                                                          Dollars

Memo:

MY SAMPLE CHECK   20

Pay to the order of: $

                                                          Dollars

Memo:

Talk with them about establishing a routine to write the check and record in the register before moving on to the next check. As your teen completes the first check successfully, they can move on to the next bill and start on the check.

Step #3: Online Bill Pay

Many of us have moved into the phase of online banking and **online bill pay**. If you use online banking it's time to introduce your teen to it too.

If you don't use online banking but have been curious, it may be time to give it a shot. We suggest you set up the bill pay process before you work with your teen. You may be surprised at how easily your teen picks up on this since they use the computer for so many things in their life already.

Take the time to go over the online banking programs and each screen explaining what you see. Be sure to show them where to find the available balance before you start paying any bills.

- Show them how to select the payee from the list you have already established.

- Show them where to enter the desired amount to pay.

- Show them how to select the date the payment will be sent.

- Discuss your personal payday and how you might want to make date selections based on the next time you get paid.

- Talk about the lag time in the online payment (although shorter than snail mail), so you don't wait until the last day to make the payment.

Step #4: A Quick Review

- Before you end your bill paying session, take a minute to go over what you and your teen have been doing. Tell them that you'd like them to help you again, so they can really get the hang of it. Also, now is a great time to just talk about bills and expenses.

- Are there any bills that they think can be lowered or eliminated altogether?.

- If every person in the household has a cell phone do they think there needs to be a home phone?

- Why do bills change from month to month? Discuss why bills fluctuate with the change in weather and in the area of the country where you live.

Step #5: Off to the Bank We Go!

Now it's time to go to the bank or credit union and open a savings and/or checking account in your teenager's own name. If they are not yet 18, you will likely be a **co-signer** on the account. That means all responsibility for the account ultimately rests with you.

At the bank, make sure the bank or credit union representative covers all the fees and restrictions with your teenager. And don't forget to ask about **overdraft protection** options.

Before you leave, take your teen to the nearest ATM and have them practice making a deposit, a withdrawal and helping them to read and understand the receipt. Remember, most teens have

DOLLARS & $ENSE

Six months before heading off to college, Jack's parents decided it was time for Jack to begin managing money. Jack's parents showed him how to use the card and how to keep track of his spending and deposits by recording his transactions in a checking account register. They also showed him the online bank record of his transactions.

Once Jack was away at school, however, he skipped the part of keeping a register, preferring to check the balance of his account online. Then the overdrafts started to appear. At first the overdrafts were occasional and Jack's parents would remind him of the importance of not over-drawing his account and they would pay the fees. But by sophomore year, that pattern became far too frequent and the parents were spending hundreds of dollars just to cover the fees. Jack's explanation was always the same: "I figure if the ATM gives me money, then I haven't overdrawn."

When Jack came home for the summer that year, his parents told him that he would not be returning to college in the fall if he didn't prove to them that he could manage his checking account responsibly and keep his register current.

That summer, Jack worked at his family's business; a wholesaler of glass bottles and containers. His duties included tracking orders, packing and shipping orders, resolving supplier and customer issues over the phone, following up on payments with customers, and generating bills. Jack had a high level of responsibility and his parents were extremely impressed with Jack's ability to handle so many details and money-related tasks! In fact, he saved them a lot money and time in many different ways.

While Jack's parents kept track of his work hours, they were reluctant to pay him on a regular basis. They were afraid that the money he earned would be spent immediately and this money was supposed to provide him with spending money for the entire upcoming school year. Therefore, Jack's parents paid him minimal amounts throughout the summer, and then paid him the remainder in one lump sum at the end.

Jack did prove to his parents that he could manage his checking account responsibly and so off to school he went that fall. But before he left, Jack's parents overheard a conversation between Jack and his girlfriend. He was boasting about how he could keep a checkbook register and always knew what his balance was in his account. To that, his college sophomore girlfriend replied, "What's a checkbook?"

never seen a bank receipt before and the terms are not familiar to them.

Next, go to a different bank or credit union ATM and have them make a withdrawal. They may be surprised to learn that they will be charged a fee from an ATM not associated with their bank or credit union. Talk about where several ATMs of their bank are located in the area and that it is always smarter to use those and avoid needless fees. (When you get home, be sure to have your teenager record in the register the deposits and withdrawals they made that day. Also have them go on line and view their account. Point out to-day's bank activities.)

Then go and grab a latte or some other treat and celebrate this first, critical step in your teenager's banking life.

While enjoying your latte, reiterate one last point: Your teen now has a debit card that can be used instead of cash or checks to make purchases at many stores and restaurants. However, since a debit card allows immediate deductions (subtrac-tions) from the checking account, **it means the money is gone!**

Step #6: "We're good, right?"
Talking about teenage money pitfalls and how to avoid them

Now is the perfect time for a quickie review. Ev-ery new job and task comes with its own 'lingo,' and it's important that your teen, that one with the hot debit card in his or her pocket, under-stand some common banking terms and their im-plications.

If you write a check and there isn't enough money in your checking account to cover the amount it is called an **overdraft**. If your bank or credit union returns the check to you the check has '**bounced**'. The bank or credit union will charge you a fee ranging from $20 – more depending on the bank and how many times you have been overdrawn before. By the way, you still owe the money to the person or business to whom you wrote the check!

Explain to your teen about the time lag that oc-curs between writing checks and having them clear the bank. Explain that even the account bal-ance online won't necessarily reflect the money available to them because of the lag. And that's why keeping a checking account register is so im-portant.

One way to prevent **overdraft fees** is to have your checking account linked to another account, such as a savings account. That way, if you don't have enough money in your checking account to cover the check you wrote, the bank will know to use funds from the savings account in order to

cover the check. You must, however, be certain that your savings account contains enough funds to help you out!

Another way to prevent overdraft fees is to sign up for **overdraft protection** at your bank or credit union. This 'protection' will allow the check to be processed, and the bank will pay the other party, but the bank will charge you fees which can add up to a lot of money if you are not careful.

Similarly, if you try to pay for something with the debit card and your account does not have the proper funds, you may be denied the purchase. This may be avoided with overdraft protection, but again, there may be substantial fees that come along with that 'protection'.

Finally, it is crucial that your teenager learn how to access their bank account online and be able to monitor the account activity. Sit with them and explain what all the terms mean and help them navigate the website. Suggest that they check their account several times per week to head off problems.

Our students love having money. Very few love the self discipline that is required to manage it successfully. They often tell us they just wish they were millionaires because then they would:

a. have enough and never need to worry about keeping track of their money, and

b. they could afford to hire someone else to manage it.

It's important to let your teenager know that even 'rich people' with accountants can get into trouble if they don't become disciplined and educated about managing their money. The following story drives this point home and it's is a good one to have your teenager read.

Step #7:
Check Back In With Your Teenager

In a month or so, sit down with your teenager and talk about the following:

- How often are they using the debit card?

- What are they purchasing with the debit card?

- Have they made any deposits?

- Have they been overdrawn at any time?

- Have any fees accumulated? For what actions?

- Have they been recording their transactions in the register?

- Do they know what their current balance is?

Don't be surprised if they aren't doing a great job. Remember, it's new to them. Developing responsible habits takes time. Talk about what they need to do to get a better handle on their finances. Tell them that you expect to see improvement in the next month. If another month passes and you see no improvement, our suggestion is to take the card away for a period of time and return to an all-cash system until they can prove to you that they are managing more responsibly.

DOLLARS & $ENSE

Darryl has been the bookkeeper for a wealthy family for years. He's paid the bills and tuition for all six of the children to attend private high schools in the Los Angeles area. Four of the kids have gone on to attend prestigious colleges while two are still in high school.

He couldn't believe the day the oldest child, Chloe, came back to her parents' house from her Laguna Beach condo with a stack of mail. Chloe just dropped her mail on Darryl's desk for him to open and take care of. After all, Darryl had always taken care of the family finances and all of Chloe's money matters while she was on the East Coast at college. The problem was that this mail had accumulated for about 2 months! There were multiple bills and second notices. Chloe hadn't paid any of her bills. She was behind on credit card bills, the mortgage, and utility bills. Her rates increased and her fees had really added up. Chloe didn't know any better.

Darryl had a talk with Chloe about how important it was to not let this happen again – that this repeated behavior would ruin her credit. Chloe didn't take it so well and seemed irritated to be lectured by "the help."

Darryl paid the bills and took care of everything but told Chloe that she should open, read, and take care of her mail on a regular basis. Chloe told Darryl that she didn't even know how to write a check. She'd never been taught that in school. Chloe's parents never paid their own bills, so they never showed her how.

Not long ago, the family's poor money management finally caught up with them. Some of "the help" had to be let go – the driver, the personal chef, and the dog walker. They even had a garage sale to raise money from seemingly endless purchases of clothing, shoes, electronics, household furnishings and more. And Chloe? Well, she is having to survive on her own. Needless to say, Chloe's beach-front condo is up for sale – she could no longer afford it and she moved home.

Chapter One Checklist:

Check off the items you and your teenager have completed:

☐ 1. Open a savings and a checking account.

☐ 2. Learn how to access and monitor bank account online.

☐ 3. Use a debit card responsibly.

☐ 4. Write checks and fill in a checking account register.

☐ 5. Pay bills online.

Notes

Chapter 2

THE GOLDEN RULE & MONEY:

Money Etiquette with Friends and Strangers

"A child educated only at school is an uneducated child."

- George Santayana

THE GOLDEN RULE & MONEY:
Money Etiquette with Friends & Strangers

GOAL: To give teens practice handling money in social situations and giving money and time to charitable causes.

Your teenager lives in a capitalist, materialistic, in-your-face consumer society. It's unfortunate, but true.   Relentless advertising images delivered on TV, magazines, movies, via the Internet as emails, Twitter, Facebook 'blasts', and on plain old-fashioned billboards make it easy for teens to get caught up in the never ending battle of wanting more, more, more. That's why at the beginning of every school year we teach a lesson called "The Golden Rule and Money". We start with a simple request: **Name some important things that money can't buy you.**

Our students take a few minutes to write down a short list and here are their most common responses:
- friendship
- respect
- love
- kindness
- family
- dignity

Next we talk about The Golden Rule, namely the idea that you should treat others as you would like to be treated. That means when it comes to money, we must remember to pay others as we ourselves would like to be paid and share our wealth with others as we would wish others to share with us. In a nutshell, this lesson teaches teens a balanced perspective when it comes to learning how to handle money and gets to the very heart of money etiquette. We should use our money, in part, to enhance those non-monetary values we cherish – friendship, respect, love, kindness, family and dignity. Whether it's about leaving a proper tip, paying your fair share of a bill or giving to a charitable organization, your teenager needs guidance when it comes to applying The Golden Rule and money in their day-to-day life.

Let's start this conversation by having you do something with your teenager that you both can get excited about – going out to eat.

DOLLARS & $ENSE

Our high school finance academy hosts "Dinner Out," a fundraiser organized by our students. Local restaurants pass along 10 - 20% of total sales for the night in return for the extra business we bring in. Recently, the students hosted a dinner night to raise funds for a field trip.

During the dinner, we were moving around from table to table chatting with our students for a minute or two and often meeting their parents for the first time. Occasionally there would be a table of just students with no adult presence.

On one of our rounds we noticed a student table had cleared out but in their wake they left french fries strewn about, half empty sodas, and traces of hot fudge sundaes. Mixed in with the evidence of a teen junk food binge was a stray dollar and a few coins. We looked at each other in horror, with the exact same thought in our head - this was their tip!

We were so embarrassed. Our students, the ones who had been learning and using financial concepts all year didn't know basic restaurant etiquette. Clearly it was time for us to step in and serve up a lesson on money etiquette. Maybe it can save a hard working waiter or waitress from getting stiffed!

Restaurant Etiquette
Step #1: Go On a Date with Your Teen!

Tipping appropriately for service is part of adult life. But teens are still new to all the rules. So, set a date to go out to lunch or dinner with your teen. Not fast food or drive thru, but a sit-down restaurant where you order and pay at the table and where you would be expected to leave a tip. Set a budget for the meal and go over the prices together. Discuss the importance of setting aside some of the budgeted funds to cover the tax and tip. Check the "Helpful Tips" in this exercise for ideas on how to calculate the tip and for a strategy to use when dining out with multiple friends.

Over the course of lunch or dinner you should talk about the activities you have completed from Chapter One and take a look at the next chapters in the book.

When the bill comes, go over all of the items and discuss tax and tip. Why do we leave a tip for a waiter or waitress? How is it calculated? Should you give 15% or 20%? Make sure your teenager understands that when they pay with cash they should always budget and set aside a 15% tip when ordering. You need to keep that in the back of your mind, so you have enough money at the end of the meal to cover the total cost – *including tip!*

"I now know how to leave the right amount for a tip. Before, I would just throw in a couple dollars no matter what the bill was."

— Agavni, age 16

- valet parking
- manicures/pedicures/spa treatments
- holiday tipping for newspaper delivery
- taxi cabs

What about other occasions where your teenager will be expected to split a bill or a charge? These may include:

- expenses that relate to special occasions such as proms and other dances (limo, restaurant)

- expenses that relate to apartment living with roommates (security deposit, utilities, furniture)

- expenses that relate to trips with friends (gas, room rental, groceries)

Restaurant Etiquette
Step #2: Figuring Out the Tip - Some Helpful Hints!

- An easy way to calculate a 15% tip is to first figure out what a 10% tip would be and then divide that in half and add it back to the original thus ending up at 15%. Remember that an easy way to figure out 10% is just $1 for every $10.

- Another way to figure out 10% is to move the decimal one place to the left. For example, if your bill total is $28.00, move the decimal one place to the left and it becomes $2.80.

Restaurant Etiquette
Step #3: Other Situations

Before you leave the restaurant, spend some time discussing other situations where tipping is appropriate. Some occasions include:

- haircuts
- pizza delivery
- bell hops at hotels

Often young people go out to eat together and have to share the bill and invariably someone gets stuck paying more than their fair share. An easy strategy to follow is to take all of the items from your personal order and round them up to the nearest dollar, then add them all together for a total. Divide that by 4 to find 25% and add that back to your original total. The 25% will give you 10% for tax (depending on your area) and 15% toward tip. That way you will not be the one always underpaying – the one who nobody wants to go out to eat with!

Now is the time to share your stories – good and bad – that involved tipping and splitting. Teens love to hear about adults making mistakes (and admitting them!) so go ahead and have some fun with it.

Let's use some real numbers here. First figure out what the tax and total would be for this receipt. Fill in your answers.

Now let's calculate just your portion of the bill. For example, you go out with a friend and order a $2.50 soda, the $2.50 side salad and the $7.00 hamburger. Add only your items and you get a total of $12.00.

What is 10%? _____
That would be your portion of the tax.

What is 15%? _____
That would be your portion of the tip.

Add it all together and that's your portion of the bill. Don't underpay because you don't know how to calculate your portion.
                    No Excuses!

Le
Fake Restaurant
Receipt
Soda 2@2.50 .. $5.00
.... $2.50
Side Salad $7.00
Hamburger $8.00
Tuna Melt..... $2.00
Ice Cream $24.50
Subtotal ..... $____
Tax @ 9.75%.. $____
Total .....

Another Easy Tip:
Sometimes it works out very easily to divide your total bill by 4 to get the 25% in one quick step. You can see how easy it would be to do this with $12.00. If you divide your total by 4 you find that you owe $3.00 toward your portion of tax and tip.

"I never really thought about how to calculate a tip because my parents don't let me look at the bill when we go out to eat. I thought a $1.00 tip per meal would be good, but I never really thought about it before."
                                                    - Mary, age 15

Changing the World

Now that your teenager knows about tipping and splitting bills with others, it's time to look at spending money and time (which is really a form of money) from a whole other perspective – giving it away. Your teenager is part of Generation Y (also known as the "Millennials"), born between 1976 and 2000. Research findings suggest that Gen Y is the most civic-minded generation to date. A higher share of Gen Y participates in community service today than ever before. An online survey conducted by Cone Inc. and AMP Insights in 2010 revealed that:

- 61% of 13-25 year olds feel personally responsible for making a difference in the world.

- 81% have volunteered in the past year.

- 69% consider a company's social and environmental commitment when deciding where to shop.

- 83% will trust a company more if it is socially or environmentally responsible.

What is causing this generation to be so generous with their time and money? Many researchers have suggested two probable causes:

1. The Internet. This generation grew up in the age of computers, the Internet, and social networking. They are more connected to what's going on globally. They are aware of problems like starvation in sub-Saharan Africa and rainforest destruction in South America, whereas generations before them had less immediate connection and thus felt less motivated to take action.

2. Competition. This generation also grew up in a highly competitive society. Many of their parents and influential adults held up college as the goal and the push was on to build their college resumé early. One way to do that is to demonstrate a consistent commitment to community service and volunteerism. Community service is now a part of the educational fabric of both public and private education – grade school, middle school, high school, and college.

Giving to a Charity
Step #1: Give of Yourself – Time, Energy, or Money

Start by having a talk with your teenager about what interests them. Is it hunger, poverty, education, animal advocacy, environmental issues? In the chart below, have your teen write down their preferences. Suggest that your teenager investigate volunteering options at his or her school. The counseling office and the college/career office can help them. There are also many teen-driven websites that allow your own teenager the opportunity to volunteer. A few that we like are:

- dosomething.org

- teenlife.com

- volunteermatch.org

- about.com – search on volunteer opportunities for teens

You can talk to other parents, students and work colleagues to get ideas. Now have your teen fill in the purpose of the group, the expected time commitment (when does the group meet and what activities are planned for the year?), and

VOLUNTEER OPPORTUNITIES AT SCHOOL

	#1	#2	#3
Causes or Charities of Interest at School			
Purpose			
Time Commitment			
Tasks/Duties You Are Expected to Perform			
Is a Money Donation Expected?			

what your teen's role will likely be in that organization. Will your teenager be expected to make a monetary donation or contribute to expenses in some way? Thinking about this information may help your teenager discern what their motives are for wanting to join. Is it purely social? Or do they truly believe in wanting to support the purpose and activities of the group? Your teen is much more likely to have a satisfying experience if their motivation is more than a social one.

If your teenager is already involved in some sort of volunteering, ask them what they like about it. Why did they choose that one? What is their role in the organization? Do they feel the group and they are making a difference? It's important that your teenager knows you are interested (not TOO interested) in what they're doing. Let them be the expert for once and share some information you may know nothing about.

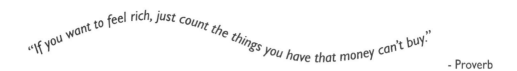

"If you want to feel rich, just count the things you have that money can't buy."

- Proverb

DOLLARS & $ENSE

As a part of the Personal Finance class at our high school, our students are required to work or volunteer for 150 hours during the summer between their junior and senior years. Here are three accounts of students' experiences as volunteer workers:

Bruno: Assistant to the Community Director of an apartment complex
While gaining valuable work experience Bruno took it upon himself to volunteer his time to help some of the employees at his job succeed at online classes they were required to pass in order to perform their jobs more effectively. "English was not their native tongue; I translated the reading material from Spanish into English and made it easier to understand. Before I got involved, their test scores were below expected requirements. After some tutoring and translating, they began to pass their tests. They started to call me "Viejo" as a term of endearment."

Mary: Hospital volunteer
"For me, making patients happy was one of the reasons why I loved volunteering so much. When a patient thanks me and compliments the way I complete my tasks, that makes me become more motivated to do better and to give the hospital 100% effort. I learned how to interact with others, follow instructions and I learned what working in the medical field is like. This made me more determined to become a doctor and the experience will help me in the future when I apply for college and apply for jobs."

Monika: Day camp/child-care volunteer
"It was scary at first starting in a new place not knowing anybody, but this volunteer experience taught me a lot. It taught me to be patient, and to interact with many different types of people. I taught the kids how to read, tell time, speak Armenian, simple geography, recycling, and various arts and crafts projects. The children would follow me everywhere hugging me and asking me to join them in playing games. My boss taught me to not be lazy, and to work a little harder to reach your goals."

Giving to a Charity
Step #2: Give Some of Your 'Stuff' Away

Your teen may decide that they have a full calendar with sports and school but still want to find a way to give back. They don't need to have money to do so. In fact, teens can go through their clothes, books, toys (electronic and otherwise) and find plenty to donate. Another great way to give back is to donate your daughter's gently used dresses or formal outfits to girls who cannot afford a dress of their own for dances or prom.

Check out www.donatemydress.org to give away that used formal dress that won't be worn again. That might inspire the whole family to get involved.   The site www.dressforsuccess.org, is a great place to donate used women's business wear or its counterpart, www.careergear.org for used men's business wear. Organizations often collect gently used sheets and towels, jackets and blankets, and adult clothing as well. There are local organizations in nearly every community that collect business wear for men and women who are getting back into the workforce.

Giving to a Charity
Step #3: Research a Good Cause

Besides giving away time and 'stuff' that benefits others and important causes, we feel it's important that teenagers begin to practice giving money away. As with any topic on money, a little education is always helpful. Let's take a minute to talk about non-profits that you and your teenager should look for when selecting a charity to support.

It's always important to do a little research on a charity to determine its legitimacy, overall financial soundness and success in achieving its mission. Make no mistake – most U.S. charities are sources of great good in our society.   They are manned with dedicated people addressing some of our most serious social issues like poverty, hunger, insufficient healthcare, housing, or education. But not all charities are created equal. In fact, the news often has eye opening reports about charities whose actual "good works" are hard to discern or whose administrative costs are so high that little money goes to the recipients the charity purports to help. In our experience, we are amazed at how many people will dig into their wallets when someone pops up at their front door claiming to raise money for a charitable cause. Our advice: take the name of the charity, its website address and promise to donate directly if you find it to be legitimate and worthy. Balancing your generosity with good common sense ensures that "charity" antics don't get under your skin and make you cynical over time.

An important thing to evaluate in charitable organizations is how much of every dollar goes into research, patient & community services and public health & education versus fundraising, management, and professional education. If the highest percent of funds goes into paying management, then there is something wrong with how that charity is being run.

Talk to your teen and tell them that being a "good financial citizen" means including charitable giving as part of life. Together discuss what charities the family has supported in the past. Someone in the family may have had direct experience with a charitable organization or perhaps suffered from an illness, one that a charity is actively involved in searching for a cure.

You may choose to keep your donation much closer to home and give to your church or place of faith. As a member, you can ask for the annual report or attend the annual meetings and see how they spend and allocate funds.

Launch the Internet and fill in the chart below:

CHARITIES AND CAUSES

	Charity or Cause #1	Charity or Cause #2	Charity or Cause #3
Purpose or mission			
Where do they operate?			
Number of members or volunteers			
How are donations distributed and used?			
Find the page that shows revenues and expenses. How large is the **Management Expenses** figure compared to the other expense figures?			

We have our students interview family members about their charitable giving. Here are a few of their thoughts:

"I never knew my grandmother donated so much money to our church. She told me that it was very important to her and she has donated every month for over 40 years."

— Amanda, age 16

"My aunt survived breast cancer and now she faithfully donates money to the Susan G. Komen Foundation. It really hit me how much that disease affects peoples' lives – even after they're cured. It made me want to find out more about the Foundation and what I could do."

— Vanessa, age 17

"My parents have sent money and used clothing to the poor in Armenia for years. I never knew they did that. It made me want to get involved in the Armenian Club at school."

— Hovakim, age 16

Giving to a Charity
Step #4: Take Action!

You and your teenager have had the talk and done some research. Now it's time to act. Have your teen answer the following:

- If not already involved, which volunteering opportunity is your teenager going to commit time to?

- When will they begin their service?

- To which charity or cause will your teenager donate?

- How much and how often?

Remember, doing for others can really make you feel good about yourself. Teens are often wrapped up in their own little world and too self-ish to fathom that ordinary people are out there who do random acts of kindness. If parents encourage their teens to participate in some sort of charity work they might find that their teen begins to see the world around them in a whole new way.

We feel it is important to start teaching about giving at an early age. After all, money isn't all about earning and spending. Still, we want to teach people to be savvy with their money, even when it comes to charitable donations. People give for many different reasons, but it's always good to know how much of every dollar goes to help the actual cause. Take the time to do a little investigating and then give with a clear conscience.

A final note: This may also be the time to let your teenager know that Uncle Sam gives taxpayers a break for giving away things and money to charitable causes. Unfortunately, most teenagers who file a tax return use the Form 1040EZ where the tax deduction for charitable donations is not allowed. (In order to take the deduction, the Form 1040, schedule A must be completed. More about these forms and how they apply to your teenager is covered in Chapter 9, *This Is Going to Hurt: Taxes and Why They Matter.*)

DOLLARS & $ENSE

Terri learned a lesson about charitable giving from her son. As she tells it, "Several years ago, I was having my car inspected and while we were in the waiting room, John — who was about 7 at the time — asked me for a nickel. I thought he'd spotted a bubble gum machine or something; however, a minute later he came back with tears in his eyes and said, "Mom, I just saved a life!"

On the cashier's counter sat a collection can for a children's charity which said, 'Giving a nickel can save a life'. He'd been moved to tears thinking that's what he'd done.

Chapter Two Checklist:

Check off the items you and your teenager have completed:

☐ 1. Discuss with your teen the meaning of the Golden Rule and how it applies to money.

☐ 2. Go on a date with your teen and teach them how to calculate the bill and figure out the tax and tip.

☐ 3. Go over each of the Helpful Tips and the Fake Restaurant Receipt Activity.

☐ 4. Discuss other occasions where tipping and splitting the bill apply.

☐ 5. Discuss volunteering and investigate an organization of your teen's choice. Fill in the chart.

☐ 6. Discuss charitable giving giving and investigate a charity or cause of your teen's choice. Fill in the chart.

☐ 7. Encourage your teenager to join a volunteer organization and make a charitable contribution

Notes

Chapter 3

PROCEED WITH EXTREME CAUTION:

Credit Card Reality

"Too many people spend money they haven't earned, to buy things they don't want, to impress people they don't like."

- Will Smith

PROCEED WITH EXTREME CAUTION: Credit Card Reality

GOAL: To give teens an understanding of how credit cards work – their advantages and pitfalls.

Let's start off this chapter by staring the monster in the face. Here are some sobering statistics on credit cards:

- According to school loan provider, Nellie Mae, more than 54 percent of college freshmen carry a credit card. By sophomore year, the percentage of students who own at least one card rises to 92 percent. Nellie Mae also reports that on average, freshmen bring an average of $1,585 in credit card debt to college.

- Seniors graduated with an average credit card debt of more than $4,100, up from $2,900 almost four years ago. Close to one-fifth of seniors carried balances greater than $7,000. (Source: Sallie Mae, "How Undergraduate Students Use Credit Cards," April 2009)

- Undergraduates are carrying record-high credit card balances. The average (mean) balance grew to $3,173, the highest in the years the study has been conducted. Twenty-one percent of undergraduates had balances of between $3,000 and $7,000, also up from the last study. (Source: Sallie Mae, "How Undergraduate Students Use Credit Cards," April 2009)

- Average credit card debt has increased 47 percent between 1989 and 2004 for 25-to 34-year-olds and 11 percent for 18- to 24-year-olds. Nearly one in five 18- to 24-year-olds is in "debt hardship," up from 12 percent in 1989. (Source: Demos.org, "The Economic State of Young America," May 2008)

DOLLARS & $ENSE

Suzy was enjoying her new-found freedom away from her parents in college. She regularly attended class but never missed a party or a chance to meet some new friends. One day while walking near the student union she spotted some really attractive frat boys. As she strutted over to their area she could see that they had some boxes of candy and simple string backpacks strewn out over a table. They called to her and she bounced over to meet them.

The young men started out telling her about the upcoming party that weekend at their frat house. They mentioned they were getting students to sign up for a credit card as a fundraiser for their fraternity. How could she say no? She told them she didn't have any source of income but mentioned that she got an allowance of $250 a month from her parents. They said that would work, so she finished up the application, got a free jumbo box of M&Ms and a reminder about the party that weekend.

As she sat through her Psychology lecture she was distracted with the idea of this new form of freedom…freedom in spending and shopping and eating out and travel and… Over the course of that year Suzy went by the mall now and again for some new threads but started to notice her clothes were getting tighter. Pretty soon her credit card was maxed out. She looked over her statements to see what she had spent $1000 on. It seemed that nearly every purchase was some sort of food. She realized she didn't have much to show for all that spending but the weight she had gained.

Suzy didn't want to tell her parents about her dumb choice and how it all happened so fast. She used her allowance to buy necessities and pay the minimum payment on her credit card, but the card balance never seemed to get any lower. The gravy train of spending ended as quickly as it started. She carried that balance for months before she could make a decent payment to make a dent in the balance. She used some of the $1,200 she earned over the summer to lower the balance, but it was right back up to being maxed out in no time after she returned for her sophomore year. This terrible cycle repeated itself over and over each year.

During her college years the credit limit on the card was extended many times until it reached $5,000. What was once a little retail therapy had become a spending addiction. Her parents never even knew she had a credit card, and she wasn't about to tell them about her predicament. It wasn't until after graduation when she was earning some decent money was she able to pay the balance down. As if a huge weight had been lifted off of her, the feeling of relief was unbelievable! Suzy decided to never fall into that trap again. She made her last payment and decided to only use the card for emergencies, and never to use the card for food purchases. She was ashamed of her decisions and wanted to just wash her hands of all that past poor judgment, so she closed her account.

We firmly believe that if you give a teenager practice using and managing a credit card before they head off to college, the odds are better that they will be more responsible at handling debt. This doesn't mean giving your teen one of your cards. Rather, this means having your teen apply for, use and manage a credit card – all under your supervision.

Most teenagers understand the concept of using plastic to make a purchase – it's easy and almost magical. What they don't fully grasp is how quickly people can get into trouble by using credit cards. The main reason for this is that people use credit cards to buy things when they don't have the money to pay for the things in the first place.

Step #1: The Language of Credit Cards
Spend some time discussing with your teenager some of the terms and concepts involved with credit cards and how they work.

- A **credit card** is a loan from a bank or credit union to purchase things now with the ability to pay back the borrowed money later.

- In the banking world, a loan is called the **principal**. On a credit card, the principal is the **credit card balance** – that's how much you owe the bank or credit union.

- There are times when using a credit card or getting a loan makes good sense. Credit cards are convenient; you don't have to carry around a lot of cash. Credit cards allow you to buy something now that may be important for you, and **pay it off over time**.

- <u>Paying it off over time is where things get tricky</u>. When banks or credit unions loan you money on credit cards, they charge interest. **Interest** is the cost of borrowing money. It is always expressed as a percent – for example, 14.5%. If you borrowed $1000 with interest charges at 14.5%, after one year, you would have to pay back the $1000 plus $145.00 for the privilege of borrowing the $1000 (1000 x 14.5% = $145.00). In the credit card world, the term **APR** (annual percentage rate) is often used, rather than "interest rate."

- People get into even more trouble when the APR (interest rate) does something called "compound." **Compound interest** is interest that applies to both the principal AND the interest of the loan. The term **APY** (annual percentage yield) is the actual annual interest rate with compounding included. It is often higher than the APR. How does that happen? It happens when you don't pay off your loan on time.

To make this process more real to your teen, take a look at one of your own credit card statements together and find:

- Name of the bank that issued the card
- APR and APY
- Credit card balance
- Minimum payment (least amount required to pay)
- Due date
- The charges listed on the statement. Talk about which charges are needs (necessities) and which charges are wants (non-necessities)
- See if your teenager can identify which charges apply to him or her

Step #2: The Big Enchilada
Understanding How Compound Interest
Works with a Credit Card

There's really no other way to get your teenager to understand the power of compound interest than to work through the numbers. Sit down together and spend the next 15 minutes or so going over the following examples.

EXAMPLE 1:

If during one month you bought $3,238.19 worth of "stuff" using a credit card, your credit card balance would be $3,238.19. When the bank or credit union sends you a statement it will show the balance. BUT it will also show a minimum payment amount of around 3%, or $97.15. This is all you're required to pay!! Wow, that's not bad - or is it?? Don't forget you really owe them $3,238.19

The bank or credit union is hoping that you only pay the minimum of $97.15 so that they can charge you compound interest on the amount that you don't pay - $3,141.04. That means that they will charge an APR of 14.9% on what you don't pay and then next month, they will charge interest again on the remaining balance and the interest from the first month. It's interest on top of interest and principal that adds up quickly and puts people into huge debt.

THE TRUE COST OF MAKING THE MINIMUM PAYMENT ON A CREDIT CARD

What is your credit card balance?	$3,238.19
What percent is used to calculate your monthly minimum payment?	3.0% times your credit card balance every month
What is the APR on your credit card?	14.9%

It will take you 172 months (14 years and 4 months) to pay off your credit card.   In that time, you will pay **$2,150.96** in interest. Did you catch that? The amount you paid in interest is over half of the original balance. Here's what the payment schedule looks like:

PAYMENT SCHEDULE

Month	Minimum Payment	Interest Paid	Principal Paid	Remaining Balance
1	$97.15	$40.21	$56.94	$3,181.25
2	$95.44	$39.50	$55.94	$3,125.32
3	$93.76	$38.81	$54.95	$3,070.36

We will skip ahead to the last 2 months of this example:

171	$10.00	$0.18	$9.82	$4.55
172	$4.61	$0.06	$4.55	$0.00

In the chart, only the minimum payment required is paid off each month. Even if you don't charge ANYTHING else on that card, it will take you 14 years and 4 months to pay off all of the original loan and all of the compound interest. You will pay roughly $5,300 for stuff that cost you $3,238.19, and it will take you 14 years to do it!

But – HOLD ON! Is the exercise you just completed "real-world?"

NO! Why not? Because most people use a credit card continually, not just one time and then never again. We had you go through that example so that you could clearly see how compound interest works and how it adds to your overall debt. Now that you understand the basics, let's look at a more realistic example:

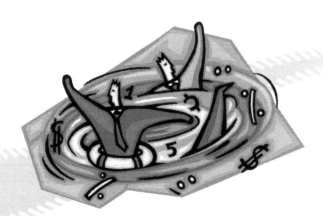

EXAMPLE 2:

The chart below shows monthly charges on a credit card with 14.9% APR, and a 3% minimum payment over 2 years.

THE "REAL" NIGHTMARE OF CREDIT CARD DEBT

Month	New Charges You Made	Credit Card Balance	14.9% APR	3% Minimum	Actual Payment Made by You	New Balance on Your Card
Sep-07	$304.00	$304.00		$9.12	$15.00	$289.00
Oct-07	$250.00	$539.00	$6.69	$16.17	$16.17	$529.52
Nov-07	$105.00	$634.52	$7.88	$19.04	$19.04	$623.37
Dec-07	$220.00	$843.37	$10.47	$25.30	$25.30	$828.54
Jan-08	$350.00	$1,178.54	$14.63	$35.36	$35.36	$1,157.81
Feb-08	$150.00	$1,307.81	$16.24	$39.23	$39.23	$1,284.82
Mar-08	$75.00	$1,359.82	$16.88	$40.79	$40.79	$1,335.91
Apr-08	$400.00	$1,735.91	$21.55	$52.08	$52.08	$1,705.38
May-08	$113.00	$1,818.38	$22.58	$54.55	$54.55	$1,786.41
Jun-08	$75.00	$1,861.41	$23.11	$55.84	$55.84	$1,828.68
Jul-08	$80.00	$1,908.68	$23.70	$57.26	$57.26	$1,875.12
Aug-08	$111.00	$1,986.12	$24.66	$59.58	$59.58	$1,951.20
Sep-08	$113.00	$2,064.20	$25.63	$61.93	$61.93	$2,027.90
Oct-08	$106.00	$2,133.90	$26.50	$64.02	$64.02	$2,096.38
Nov-08	$560.00	$2,656.38	$32.98	$79.69	$79.69	$2,609.67
Dec-08	$120.00	$2,729.67	$33.89	$81.89	$81.89	$2,681.68
Jan-09	$108.00	$2,789.68	$34.64	$83.69	$83.69	$2,740.62
Feb-09	$96.00	$2,836.62	$35.22	$85.01	$85.01	$2,786.75
Mar-09	$105.00	$2,891.75	$35.91	$86.75	$86.75	$2,840.90
Apr-09	$95.00	$2,935.90	$36.45	$88.08	$88.08	$2,884.28
May-09	$143.00	$3,027.28	$37.59	$90.82	$90.82	$2,974.05
Jun-09	$300.00	$3,274.05	$40.65	$98.22	$98.22	$3,216.48
Jul-09	$440.00	$3,656.48	$45.40	$109.69	$109.69	$3,592.19
Aug-09	$143.00	$3,735.19	$46.38	$112.06	$112.06	$3,669.51
Totals	**$4,562.00**		**$619.65**		**$1,512.14**	

As you can see, after two years and making only the minimum payment each month, you have charged $4,562 to your credit card. You have paid a total of $1,512.14 of which $619.65 is interest. So, actually you haven't made much of a dent in your balance. On August 9, you still owe $3,669.51. And the hole will just get deeper and deeper.

How can you avoid this pattern?

- Don't buy anything without having the cash to pay it off when the bill comes. It's an excellent way to build credit without acquiring debt.

- Sometimes we need items that we don't have all the money for right now. For example, a new sofa. For an expensive item such as this, force youself to save up to at least half of an item's price before charging the other half on the credit card.

- Any time you use a card to purchase something that you cannot fully payoff when the bill comes, make it a rule that you won't buy another thing until you've paid off that item in full.

- If you cannot pay off the card in full, at least pay more than the minimum payment. You will save yourself hundreds of dollars in interest.

More Danger Ahead: Fees and Charges

Our students are always shocked to learn about all the numerous fees and charges that can apply with credit cards – also known as **finance charges**. Be sure and review the following with your teenager:

- **Interest Charges**: The APR (percent) applied to any balance that is not paid in full by the due date.

- **Over-the-Limit-Fee**: A fixed amount charged when the cardholder charges more than their credit limit. This can range from a

DOLLARS & $ENSE

Class was over and Damaris, a soft spoken but forthright girl, approached the teacher. She wanted to know what would happen to her credit history and credit score if her mother used her – Damaris's - credit card and didn't make regular payments. Damaris told me that since she had recently turned 18, she had been offered a few cards and that her mother was trying to get her to apply for one so that she could use it.

I asked her why her mother would use her daughter's card, instead of her own. Apparently, Damaris's mother had maxed out her own cards and needed access to more credit for basic purchases. I explained that yes, Damaris's credit history and score would be affected by any transactions from any credit card in her name. With disappointment in her eyes, Damaris responded, "I figured it would." I asked Damaris what she was going to do next. Without hesitation she offered, "I'm not getting any credit cards right now and when I do, my mother won't know about it. She's screwed up her own life, she's not going to screw up mine."

few dollars to hundreds of dollars depending on how far you go over.

- **Late Fee**: A fixed amount charged if your payment is late.

- **Cash Advance Fee**: A fixed amount charged when the card is used to obtain cash.

Step #3: Playing With Live Ammo
Have Your Teenager Apply For a Credit Card and Begin Using It.

We know; it's a scary thought – your teen with a piece of plastic in their own name! But we recommend that a teenager start using and managing a credit card by the beginning of their senior year of high school. This will give them a year's worth of practice before they set off on their own.

Go with them to their bank or credit union and meet with a bank representative. Have them explain in the detail the credit card options and restrictions for your teen. Many banks have beginner credit cards with low credit limits that your teenager may qualify for. If not, most credit unions have teen-friendly programs and for a minimum deposit of $5.00 in to an account, will allow your teen to get started with a credit card. Again, the important thing to remember is let your teenager actually fill out the forms and make the application in person. **Don't do it for them.**

Once the credit card is issued, discuss with your teen the rules around their use of the card. We suggest the following:

- Use the card only when the purchase is pre-approved by you, the parent. You may consider having your teen use the card for purchases such as pre-approved clothing, education-related items (books, supplies), emergencies (flat tire), a class ring. For all other incidental purchases like food, movies, make-up, your teenager should use their debit card or cash.

- Have your teenager (and you) check the account activity on line each week. Discuss any discrepancies you feel need to be addressed BEFORE the monthly statement arrives.

- Every month, review the credit card statement with your teenager and stress the importance of paying the balance in full.

- Decide how much money you, the parent, should transfer into your teen's checking account to be used toward payment of the card's balance. We suggest that the teen write the check or make the online bill payment themselves – don't do it for them.

- If your teenager abuses the privilege of the card, take it from them for a month or two to **send a clear message that credit is, in fact, a privilege, not a right!**

- You might also consider a month with no restrictions - a month where you let your teen buy their everyday items on the credit card. We recommend a discussion about not going hogwild with the card, but it would be a good lesson to see how everyday spending can add up on a credit card. If they can't cover the entire monthly bill then they will have to pay interest on some of those simple everyday items. It's a great time to talk about how interest on a latte or pizza just isn't worth it in the long run!

Dollars & $ense

Raymond and Steven are partners who used to live "a little too high on the hog". In 2005 they were making a combined income of roughly $100,000 a year as teachers in the Los Angeles area. On a weekly basis, Raymond and Steven spent money on new clothes, books, and movies. But even more money was spent daily eating out – and we're not talking fast food, but most times at nice, sit-down restaurants.

It was Raymond's responsibility to pay the bills and periodically, Raymond got notices that their bank was raising the limit on the overdraft protection associated with their checking account. This was "helpful" considering Raymond and Steven were often spending more than was in their account. Unfortunately, they were assessed fees every time they needed the protection and these added up to hundreds of dollars every month.

Raymond was beginning to stress out over the amount of credit card debt they were accumulating. They didn't have enough money to pay their income taxes. The couple took out a second mortgage on their home in order to help pay for their debts. Then, Steven lost his job. To make matters worse, their home needed $9,000 in plumbing repairs and Raymond had to borrow the money from his dad. Raymond wasn't sleeping, his health began to fail, he became depressed. The partners were fighting. Their total debt: $100,000.

One Sunday, Steven noticed an article in the New York Times about credit counseling and how it had helped many people dig out from under their debts. The article offered a list of free counseling sessions offered by non-profit organizations. Steven made the appointment the next day and, together, the couple took the first step.

Fast forward to 2010. Raymond and Steven work 3 jobs - each. They save all their receipts in a stack as a reminder of what they spend money on. They talk about bills and upcoming purchases and other expenses. Rather than going to the movies, they wait until movies came out in DVD. They still go out for a good restaurant meal once in a while, but now they wait for special occasions. "Waiting, said Raymond, "makes it feel special." Raymond is eating better, sleeping better and feeling better. As he puts it, "I feel empowered and hopeful and we were doing this together."

Unlike the old days, Raymond and Steven use only one credit card. With coaching from the credit counseling sessions, they learned how to negotiate lower interest rates on some of their existing credit cards and are slowly paying them off. Raymond estimates it will take another five years to pay down the credit card debt.

Author's Note: After completing this interview, the authors couldn't help but think about all the sacrifice and hard work yet to be done. Five years is a long time for most people to work 3 jobs and scrutinize every penny made and spent. So think about this story the next time you want to make a purchase with money you don't already have sitting in the bank.

Step #4: The Adult Report Card
- Your Credit Score

Finally, now is the time to talk to your teenager about building a good **credit history** and **credit score**. Our students have all heard about a credit score and they are anxious to know how they can achieve a high score quickly. Let them know that credit card companies will pass along key information about how your teen uses and manages the card. If they use the card responsibly; pay it off on time, pay more than the minimum amount, stay under the credit limit, and use it regularly, they will begin to build their credit history and from that history, a credit score. It is also important to tell your teenager that a good credit score – 720 and above – will allow them to get the best interest rates (lowest) and access to larger amounts of credit. This will be important when the time comes for them to buy a car or home, for example.

Everyone may check their credit report for free once every 12 months from each of the nationwide consumer credit reporting companies (also known as credit bureaus), Equifax, Experian and TransUnion. For finding out your credit score from any of these companies you will be charged a minimal fee. We recommend that you and your teenager check their credit report and credit score at least once before they leave for college. Go to www.annualcreditreport.com to learn how. Remember, building good credit takes time and responsible behavior. It's serious business.

Check out this table below with your teen and discuss the correlation between the dedication and commitment it takes to school work as it does to your spending habits.

GPA to Credit Score – Expected Interest Rate

Based on your credit rating		
A	800—850 SCORE	6%
A-	750—799 SCORE	7%
B+	700—749 SCORE	8%
B-	650—699 SCORE	9%
C+	625—649 SCORE	11%
C-	600—624 SCORE	13%
D	550—599 SCORE	15%
F	BELOW 550 SCORE	NO LOAN
A	3.8 + GPA	
A-	3.5—3.79 GPA	
B+	3.25—3.49 GPA	
B-	3.00—3.24 GPA	
C+	2.75—2.99 GPA	
C-	2.25—2.74 GPA	
D+	1.90—2.24 GPA	
D	1.75—1.89 GPA	
F	1.74 OR LOWER	

Source: Mike Martin

My GPA is _____ therefore my credit score is _____

and therefore I can expect an interest rate of _____.

Teens have been students for years and know how much work it takes to get and keep good grades. They probably also know how much work it takes to repair low grades. Don't let them make the same mistake with their credit score. They now have the tools and information! Start spending wisely!

Chapter Three Checklist:

Check off the items you and your teenager have completed:

- ☐ 1. Learn the terms associated with credit cards.

- ☐ 2. Understand the concept of compound interest and how it works against you.

- ☐ 3. Understand some ways to avoid getting into credit card debt.

- ☐ 4. Apply for a credit card.

- ☐ 5. Begin using a credit card.

- ☐ 6. Manage and monitor the credit card activity.

- ☐ 7. Check their credit report and credit score before they leave for college.

Useful Websites:

- www.bankrate.com
  Useful information about credit cards and provides a credit card calculator to help manage your credit card balance.

- www.annualcreditreport.com
  The government sponsored website that explains how to view your credit report for free.

Notes

SECTION II

Preface

MAPPING OUT THE ROAD TO COLLEGE
AND TECHNICAL SCHOOL AND BEYOND

The next three chapters will take you and your teen through the financial complexities of acquiring a college or technical school education. Our advice – Be patient. Each chapter will take time and effort to complete. But at the end, you and your teen will have a much stronger sense of the financial implications – both costs and benefits – of a college or technical school education.

Remember, our focus here is to provide you with the tools to make a well-reasoned **financial** decision. We understand that your choice may not be limited solely to cost and we recognize there are many reasons why a student and their family seek out a specific school. Sending your teen to college or technical school is a complex decision with many aspects. However, while middle class household incomes have been relatively stagnant since 1970, the increase in college and technical school tuition in the U.S. has outstripped most other expenses, including housing and auto costs. According to The College Board (www.collegeboard.org) tuition and fees at four-year state universities have increased by a factor of 15 for in-state students and by a factor of about 24 for out-of-state students over the past 40 years. The Cornell College Chronicle (www.news.cornell.edu) reports that the average tuition at private universities jumped 474% from 1970 to 1990, compared with the CPI's increase of 248%.

The bottom line is that the college 'bite' is bigger now than ever before. So it's time to be a savvy shopper. Do the research, work the numbers, keep a cool head and then make a well-informed decision. You won't regret it.

Chapter 4

WHERE'S YOUR PASSION?:

Research Careers, What They Pay,
& the Skills & the Education You Need to be Successful

"Just don't give up trying to do what you really want to do.
Where there's love and inspiration
I don't think you can go wrong."

- Ella Fitzgerald

WHERE'S YOUR PASSION?:

Research Careers, What They Pay, & the Skills & the Education You Need to be Successful

GOAL: To show teens the link between doing what they love, the preparation it takes, and what they can earn.

What do you think you want to be when you grow up? For some teens it's an easy question. They've wanted to be a doctor, teacher, lawyer, or engineer as long as they can remember. But for others, many others, the answer can be a bit hazy. Some may not have a great grasp of their strengths and weaknesses. Some aren't sure how to pursue what they love and worry that they won't be able to make a good living. Some teens just don't feel ready to choose. That's not surprising. Choosing a profession is a big step, one of the bigger decisions we make in life. Help! Is there a way to make it easier?

Well, we believe in the educated hunch. Now is the time for you and your teenager to do a little research. What careers sound interesting? What sound like fun? What seem like a good fit for your teen's talents?

Whether your teenager has college aspirations, prefers to enter the workforce immediately af-

ter high school or is thinking about some other alternative, now is a great time to explore possible careers together. Many teens will find their initial 'dream career' a little less rosy upon close examination. In fact, our students' first choice of career often changes after they've spent some time researching a variety of professions. Sometimes a little research can make all the difference in the world.

Now is a great time for a teenage to imagine. After all, the world is full of possibility and they are full of potential. And really, "research" is just a fancy word for taking a good look around you. Open up. Think big picture. Researching careers can kick start teens into thinking about their future in new ways and help them map out their next steps.

Dollars & $ense

The clock said 10am and Eliza wasn't ready for work. She was still in her jammies finding all kinds of excuses not to get dressed. This was becoming a habit. Just last week, Eliza met a friend for lunch and 'clocked out' at noon. She knew she needed to make a change.

Eliza was a sales rep for a well known office equipment company. Her job was to make appointments with existing customers and potential new customers to sell or lease new office equipment like copiers, fax machines and printers. This was Eliza's first real job after college and she was proud to land a well-paying position with a prestigious company at twenty two. The "well-paying" part had one hitch though; she was paid 100% on commission (a percent of the sales she made). In other words, Eliza only made money if she sold her company's products. This required persistence, a regular routine and lots of sales calls every day.

But as the months rolled by, Eliza's enthusiasm for her job began to wane. She was bored asking people the same sorts of questions every day; "Does your copier effectively handle your current workload?" "When does your current lease finish on that fax machine?" "How much are you currently spending a month on outside copying?"

Eliza had a hard time with the constant rejection too. It took a lot of "No's" before she got a "Yes". The reported ratio was 50:1. Eliza also felt strangely alone. Although she spoke to many people throughout the day, the conversations weren't all that interesting or productive.

Pretty soon Eliza found more and more excuses for not making sales calls and her performance, her self-esteem, and her income began to suffer. It was time for her to get some help.

Eliza heard about a career counseling place that helped you identify your talents, skills and interests and the types of careers that best suited you. She made an appointment, took the tests and to her surprise, found that sales was not a good fit.

She began researching careers that were better aligned with her strengths. She realized that she needed additional education, which she promptly got, and soon found a job as a corporate analyst for an international retail company. Eliza flourished. She loved working with data and people, figuring out solutions to all kinds of different, complex business problems. That feeling lasted for years and led to advancement opportunities. Not only was she able to support herself, she actually saved and invested money throughout her 20s.

Eliza learned a life-long lesson:
If you have a passion for your work, the opportunities and rewards will follow.

Step #1: It Pays to Learn!

Education is clearly related to earnings. The more education you complete the greater salary you can potentially earn. Take a look at the statistics in the charts below.

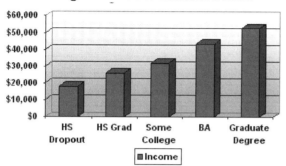

Average Income Per Education Level

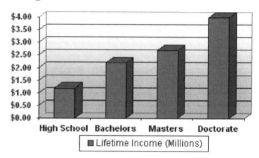

Average Lifetime Income Per Education Level

Source: Bureau of Labor Statistics

DOLLARS & $ENSE

Natalie has attended private schools her whole life. She's a senior now and applying like mad to colleges. She's always been very mature for her age and always more serious about school than her peers. She comes from a family of educators as far back as her great-grandmother, so when she says she has decided to be a math teacher her parents know she won't change her mind.

She seems to have her heart set on a private college somewhat close to home but where she can still live on campus. The grand total for her freshman year of school (minus the $5,000 scholarship they have offered her) will still set the family back about $42,000.   It's possible that a four year stint will cost Natalie and her family upwards of $160,000 and if she attains her teaching credential, Natalie might need another year, raising the full cost to $200,000! A good portion of that cost will be financed with debt since Natalie's twelve years in private school absorbed much of the family's available cash; money that could have been saved for college.

It's time to consider Natalie's educational expenses vs. her potential future income. According to the Bureau of Labor Statistics, the median annual wages of kindergarten, elementary, middle, and secondary school teachers ranged from $47,100 to $51,180 in May 2008; the lowest 10 percent earned $30,970 to $34,280; the top 10 percent earned $75,190 to $80,970. Natalie's school choice may mean shouldering a serious loan repayment burden in the future and take a big chunk out of her paycheck. Should Natalie look into less expensive colleges?

Step #2: Get a Little Perspective

The previous charts clearly show the relationship between education and earnings. However, most teens don't understand how yearly income relates to a standard of living. That's possibly because a standard of living is often expressed in our society as "social class," a complex notion reaching beyond actual income and involving our perceptions and desires.

Now is the time for your teenager to know the family's standard of living. This helps them compare how they are living now against the lifestyle they may desire in the future. Knowing what standard of living they want can help teens map out clearer educational steps to get there or alternatively, what trade-offs they may face between doing what they love and the standard of living they can expect from it.

Personal Income and Education of Individuals 25+

Social Class	Job Type	Average Income Level	Average Education Level
The Rich	CEOs, Politicians	$200,000+	Graduate Degree
Upper Middle Class	Professionals	$72,500 - $200,000	Graduate Degree
Lower Middle Class	Professional Support and Sales	$32,000 - $72,500	Bachelor's Degree
Working Class	Clerical, Service and Blue Collar	$15,000 - $32,000	Some College
Lower Class	Part-time and Unemployed	$7,000	High School

Sources: Thompson & Hickey, Society in Focus 2005, US Census Bureau Personal Income & Education of Individuals 25+, 2005

Note: Let your teen know about the term 'poverty threshold' (aka poverty line or poverty level), the amount that determines government benefits such as food stamps and welfare payments. According to the 2009 US Census Bureau, the poverty threshold for an individual was $11,161 and $21,954 for a household of four.

Your teenager should also understand that income levels are different across the country because the cost of living varies. For example, it costs a lot more money to live in New York City, than it does to live in Milwaukee, Wisconsin. That's because more people want to live in New York than in Milwaukee and there are more jobs options in New York. With more people needing apartments, homes, grocery stores and restaurants in New York, the prices of those things are higher. In order for people to pay for those higher priced items, businesses have to pay their employees more money. The following chart illustrates the median (middle) family income by state. Find your state and compare it to the others.

Median Family Income
(In 2008 Inflation-Adjusted Dollars)

#	State	Average (Family of 4)
1	New Jersey	$103,261
2	Connecticut	$102,124
3	Maryland	$101,803
4	Massachusetts	$99,648
5	New Hampshire	$93,926
6	Hawaii	$91,483
7	Delaware	$88,725
8	Rhode Island	$87,002
9	Minnesota	$86,637
10	Virginia	$85,939
11	Alaska	$85,422
12	Washington	$82,716
13	New York	$82,457
14	Colorado	$81,644
15	Illinois	$81,465
16	Wisconsin	$80,530
17	California	$79,477
18	Pennsylvania	$77,867
19	Wyoming	$79,964
20	North Dakota	$75,140
21	Michigan	$74,824
22	Vermont	$74,163
23	Ohio	$73,301
24	Iowa	$72,961
25	Oregon	$72,667
26	Kansas	$72,610
27	Nebraska	$72,542
28	Nevada	$71,104
29	Missouri	$71,059
30	Indiana	$70,873
31	Maine	$70,374
32	South Dakota	$70,182
33	Utah	$69,990
34	Arizona	$69,452
35	Florida	$69,009
36	Georgia	$68,502
37	North Carolina	$67,295
38	Texas	$66,381
39	Louisiana	$66,256
40	Montana	$65,827
41	South Carolina	$65,655
42	Alabama	$65,311
43	Kentucky	$64,459
44	Tennessee	$64,228
45	Idaho	$62,051
46	Oklahoma	$62,037
47	District of Columbia	$60,418
48	Mississippi	$58,518
49	West Virginia	$58,479
50	Arkansas	$57,905
51	New Mexico	$55,561
52	Puerto Rico	$27,532

Source: US Census 2010

DOLLARS & $ENSE

In his junior year of high school, Troy took advantage of a job shadowing opportunity at a well known, national brokerage firm. He spent an entire morning with Frank, a financial advisor. Troy observed the way Frank spoke with clients over the phone, advising them about various investments and answering questions. "He seemed to really enjoy talking with his clients and they seemed to trust him because he placed a lot of orders that day." Troy learned that it took a variety of skills to be a financial advisor, "You have to communicate well, do a lot of math in your head and work with people in different positions to get your orders completed. It seemed like an exciting job, one that would never get boring." By the end of the day, Troy and Frank had established a strong rapport – so strong in fact that Frank offered Troy an internship position once he had completed 2 years of college. Frank explained to Troy that he wanted him to have a bit more perspective on his future direction before they both invested the time and resources for a paying internship. This seemed reasonable to Troy and during the next two years of college he thought more deeply about working as a financial advisor.

Troy's studies and interests led him to focus on a combined marketing and finance path. After that second year of college, rather than taking Frank up on his offer, Troy opted for an internship with a public relations firm as a financial analyst. Although at first it was unpaid and part time, he was soon added to the payroll and eventually began working full time – finishing his college degree more slowly. In a presentation Troy recently made to our students, "Even though I didn't take advantage of the internship at the financial advisory firm, I have always been grateful for that job shadow. It opened up my eyes."

Step #3: A Little Research Won't Hurt

Now that your teenager has a better idea of how income relates to social class and education level, sit with your teen, launch the internet and begin your research. The Occupational Outlook Handbook, published by the Bureau of Labor Statistics, provides a wealth of information about jobs and careers such as:

- the training and education needed
- earnings
- expected job prospects
- what workers do on the job
- working conditions

To get started go to: www.bls.gov/oco/ . Research three careers that interest your teenager and provide the income that will support the lifestyle they are looking for.

Some Important Terms:

A **salary** is an annual amount you earn for full-time employment regardless of any extra work you do over and above your scheduled hours.

An **hourly wage** is the amount you earn for each hour you work. You do have the option to earn overtime if you work more than 40 hours a week.

RESEARCH THREE DIFFERENT CAREERS THAT INTEREST YOU

Go to: www.bls.gov/oco/

	CAREER 1
Career Name	
Training / Education Needed	
Estimated Earnings: Starting and Median	
Expected Job Prospects	
What Workers Do	
Working Conditions	

CAREER 2	CAREER 3

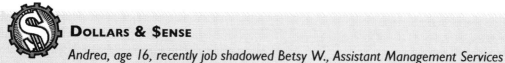

DOLLARS & $ENSE

Andrea, age 16, recently job shadowed Betsy W., Assistant Management Services Director for the City of Burbank, California. The department provides services in the areas of human relations, labor relations and safety for the employees of the City. "I thought the job shadow would be kind of boring, just sitting in her office listening to her talk about her job. But it wasn't like that at all. Betsy took me with her everywhere in the building. She introduced me to everyone no matter what their job was. I was able to meet the whole department. I even sat in on a couple of meetings she had. Betsy had so much going on and so many details to take care of. I was amazed. She was able to answer every question I had. It was a really good experience."

Step #4: Now Find Out More –
Job Shadowing, Informational Interviews and Internships

It's helpful to read about different careers and understand what it takes to pursue them. But it's even better to talk to real people on the job and hear firsthand about how they got to where they are. Better yet is to work in an environment and receive valuable training and insight about how particular jobs function within a given career. Our students participate in three experiences that broaden their understanding of careers and how to pursue certain options.

The first experience is known as job shadowing. **Job shadowing** is where students literally follow a worker as he or she performs a job. Students gain detailed perspective about the day-to-day tasks and duties of a profession and can ask questions and get immediate feedback.

Often times the student and the worker develop a special rapport that may help the student possibly secure a job or internship opportunity down the road.

To get the most out of a job shadowing experience, preparation is critical. Here are some points to consider:

• Be sure your teenager is interested in the job they will shadow! You want them to be engaged, enthusiastic and leave a good impression with the person they are shadowing.

• Your teenager should make up a list of potential questions they can ask the worker throughout the day. Questions like "How did you get started in this career?" or "How much education did you need" are two good examples. Your teen may carry the list of questions in a nice looking notebook throughout the day and make notes as they wish.

- Dress to impress. Depending on the work environment, your teenager should go to the job shadow dressed professionally. If the workplace or the job is very casual then it may be appropriate for your teenager to dress casually, but it's far better to err on the side of dressing formally and conservatively.

- Say Thank You! At the end of the day, your teenager must remember to thank the worker and any other helpful employees. Then, a teen should follow up immediately with a letter or hand written thank-you note. Be sure it arrives within a few days.

Note: For more detailed information about the points mentioned above, refer to Chapter Seven, *Carry a Toolkit: Career Readiness Essentials.*

Your teen's school may have an established job shadowing program. Check with the counseling or career office at the junior high or high school. If not, your teenager needs to expend some effort to find their own job shadowing opportunity. Have him check with neighbors, friends' parents, your friends, and relatives to see if he could shadow them at work sometime. Very motivated students may contact an individual by writing a letter. Adults are often very sympathetic to a teenager's interest and initiative and will accommodate a stranger's request. **But no matter what, let your teen do the legwork and own the process. Don't set up a job shadow for them!**

DOLLARS & $ENSE

Valente, a high school junior, conducted an informational interview over the phone. His interviewee, Dr. Kristin Waters, principal of Bruce Randolph Middle School in Denver, Colorado is credited with turning the state's worst performing middle school into one of its top performers. Valente had first learned of Dr. Waters through President Obama's State of the Union Address in 2011 in which the President praised her efforts in educational innovation. Valente had a number of friends who had dropped out of high school and he wondered how someone could really change a school enough to motivate kids to stay and graduate. After some online research, Valente found Dr. Waters work phone number and called her to set up a phone interview. "Dr. Waters inspired me by telling me what she did to turn around the school. She impressed upon me the idea that even if no one believes in you, never give up. Go for what makes you happy."

The second experience is known as the informational interview. An **informational interview** is just that – an interview where you gain information about a job, career, industry or company. It is not a job interview. Instead you speak with someone working in a profession you're interested in. Our students are required to conduct informational interviews. They research jobs of interest and then use their own contacts to find and set up an informational interview. Again, your school may have the resources to help your teenager. But if not, the teen will need to exploit their contacts and they may need your help in the process. **Don't set up the interview for them. It's important that they make the phone call or write the letter and follow up.**

Just like the job shadow, your teen must be prepared for the interview. They should:

- Do research
- Make a list of questions
- Dress to impress
- Say thank you

Internships offer another way for teens to learn about a profession. An internship is any period of time during which a beginner acquires experience in an occupation, profession, or pursuit. An internship may be paid or unpaid. It may last a short period of time, perhaps just a summer, or it may last several years. Some companies and organizations offer formal programs on a regular basis and others do not. Individuals within the organization may even set-up an internship based on their particular needs or from the desire to help a deserving and motivated young person. Corporations, small companies, non-profit organizations, and government agencies are all possible venues for internships. Your teenager should first decide which careers are of interest to him or her and then do some research to figure out which organizations to approach.

Our students consistently report that one of the most meaningful aspects of high school and college was the internship experience. Being an intern answers a lot of questions about careers and workplace environments and gives teens something very valuable to add to their growing resume. An internship can also lead to a full-time

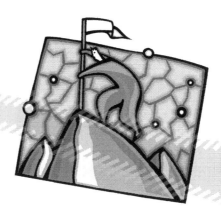

position. In that case there is the added benefit of knowing in much greater detail what kind of organization you are joining as a full-time employee. Your teenager should check to see if their high school or college has an established internship program. If not, your teen will have to network (and do some footwork!) to uncover an internship position for themselves. Some useful websites include:

www.internshipratings.com

www.internships.com

www.internshipprograms.com

Applying for an internship is very similar to applying for a job. The only real difference is that an internship is temporary – usually with an agreed upon start date and end date. And just like applying for a job, your teenager will most likely need a resume, cover letter, and reference page. Additionally, they will most likely participate in the interview process. In Chapter Seven, *Carry a Toolkit: Career Readiness Essentials*, the relevant documents and tips on interviewing are covered in detail. We recommend that you and your teenager review Chapter Seven to increase their chances of landing an internship.

Step #5: Debrief With Your Teenager

You and your teenager have researched several careers – what they are about, qualifications needed, and what they pay. You've talked about job shadowing, informational interviews and internships. Wow, that's a lot. Take a moment to talk all this over with your teenager. How's your teen feeling about it all? Chances are they may be enthusiastic but a bit overwhelmed. Have a brief conversation with your teenager to see where their interest lies at this time. Has this section of the book sparked new ideas? Pay attention to what your teenager is telling you. Let them know you are there to support them as they explore these first steps into their adult life. Often, just listening and validating their feelings is enough to give them confidence to make the next move.

Chapter Four Checklist:

Check off the items you and your teenager have completed:

☐ 1. Look over the degree and average annual earnings table.

☐ 2. Discuss how standards of living, educational level, and income relate to one another.

☐ 3. Research three different careers online.

☐ 4. Complete at least one job shadow experience.

☐ 5. Complete at least one informational interview.

☐ 6. Research at least one internship opportunity.

☐ 7. Debrief with your teenager.

Notes

Chapter 5
THE REAL COST OF EDUCATION:

Loans, Grants, & Scholarships for College & Technical School

"An investment in knowledge pays the best interest."

- Unknown

THE REAL COST OF EDUCATION:
Loans, Grants, & Scholarships for College & Technical School

GOAL: To learn about different sources of money to help pay for higher education. Connect the dots between the cost of education, debt repayment, and potential future earnings. Together, develop a plan for financing your teenager's education.

If your teenager is going to college or vocational school immediately after high school, you know that the financial cost can be high. Even if your teen decides to enter the workplace, there is still a good chance that additional education at a college or vocational school is in their future. No matter what your teen's situation is today, it is highly beneficial that they understand the cost of education and how to pay for it.

DOLLARS & $ENSE

From the time Kelly was 6 years old she knew she wanted to work with animals. From Red-light Sally her tabby cat, to Sam her rescue mutt, Kelly tirelessly nurtured each one of her twelve family pets over the years. In fifth grade, Kelly started Kelly's Canine Company – a pet sitting service she continues to operate today. "Once when I was twelve," recalls Kelly, "a bunny died in my care. That experience taught me to cherish animals because they live especially short lives."

As a teenager, Kelly interned and volunteered at several pet hospitals and at the largest no-kill animal sanctuary in the U.S., Best Friends Animal Sanctuary. "This organization stands for what I want to do with my life. They see the promise in all animals," says Kelly.

Throughout high school Kelly maintained excellent grades, earned high test scores and pursued meaningful extra-curricular animal-related experiences. She applied to numerous veterinarian and pre-vet programs throughout the country. While her parents wanted the best for Kelly, they were caught in a frustrating situation; they made too much money for Kelly to qualify for government grants and work study programs but not enough to pay for many of the programs Kelly was interested in. That is, not unless they wanted to dip into retirement savings or sell their home – not very realistic or prudent options. They still had other children at home, and like many parents, were living in the aftermath of the great recession and coping with diminished retirement savings and investment accounts.

Kelly knew that she had her work cut out for her. In addition to tackling time consuming college applications she had to research every financial aid option possible.

Kelly's top choice for vet school was Colorado State University, but as a Californian, she would be an out-of-state-student obligated to pay much higher tuition than in her home state. Undeterred, Kelly discovered this school was part of the Western Undergraduate Exchange program which allows students from certain states to receive a reduction in tuition. In her case, she would be required to pay Colorado's in-state tuition times a half, not the usual two to four times out-of-state-rate that most schools charge.

With a little more research and help from the university's vet school, Kelly received a one-time Presidential Scholarship Award of $1000. She also qualified for the vet school honors program at CSU and received $2,000 per year and $3,000 from the Vet Start Program. For her part, Kelly must maintain a 3.0 and earn 12 credits per semester.

According to Kelly's mother, "These awards brought her CSU tuition lower than the best in-state school Kelly was admitted to. It sure made out-of-state tuition less scary."

Kelly was thrilled to receive these awards though she knew there were dozens of other available community-based scholarships that she didn't apply for. The whole college application process had worn her down and she just couldn't write one more essay or fill out one more application. Kelly's advice: "Have a plan for researching and applying for scholarships before applying for college. Know that you will have a lot of work to do even AFTER you finish the college application process."

Step #1: Listen and Learn

Take a few moments to review your teenager's career preferences and the education needed from Chapter 4, *Where's Your Passion?* Then ask your teen what colleges or vocational schools they know of that offer degrees or certifications in those careers. If they have no idea, suggest a few schools to kick off their search.

With two or three schools in mind, now go to those schools' websites and, with your teen, research the degrees, certifications, tuition, fees, and your teenager's general 'feeling' about the schools' websites – a possible gauge of whether or not your teen may feel comfortable going to that school.

Don't freak out at the eye-popping costs! The second half of this lesson provides information about how to pay for school and plan ahead. Use the chart on the next page to keep track of the information you discover along the way.

Completing the chart is a good start on your journey. Feel free to expand the chart, adding additional schools you and your teen may want to explore.

After you're done with the chart, take a break. But don't forget to come back and finish this lesson because the next part will help you figure out how to pay for an education that could set your teenager up for a satisfying and successful future.

Youlen, a student and a Girl Scout leader, told us that at one of her meetings she had all the girls in her troop create a college research chart and fill it in. "I learned so much by doing this in class that I wanted to share this with all of them. It was fun and they learned alot, too."

EDUCATION RESEARCH

Name of College or Vocational School	City, State	Is the Type of Degree or Certification You Seek Offered?	Cost of Tuition	Other Fees (Room/board, meal plan, books, other)

Step #2: Where's the Money?
Discuss with your teenager the differences between grants, work-study, scholarships, and student loans.

When it comes to paying for college or technical school, the costs are often staggering! Some parents have little or no money to contribute. Others may have savings to put toward their child's education and a (very) few can afford to pay for education out of their checking account. Most parents find that it takes a combination of many sources to cover the costs. This can range from student loans, grants, scholarships, teenager contributions, parent contributions, and even grandparent contributions. The important thing to remember is that with some research, hard work, and planning, you and your teenager can find a way to make it happen.

Most teenagers have no idea about all the different programs and options available to help pay for school. Many parents don't either. Often times it is parents who handle all of this 'behind the scenes' and the teenager goes off to school with no appreciation of how their studies will be financed. That's a well-intentioned mistake! Understanding the cost of education is another crucial step in a teenager's growth toward financial independence. So don't hide any of this from them.

Federal Student Aid Grants:
A **grant** is financial aid that *doesn't* have to be repaid. That's right, it's FREE money! Currently, there are 6 Federal Student Aid Grants available. Generally speaking, most of these grants are awarded to students with exceptional financial need and may contribute thousands of dollars toward a degree or program. As with all Federal Aid programs, you and your teenager must complete the Free Application for Federal Student Aid (FAFSA) application to determine if your teenager is eligible for a Federal Student Aid Grant. Go to: studentaid.ed.gov for all the details.

Federal Work-Study (FWS) Program:
The FWS Program allows your student to work part-time while going to school to pay for some of their education. Many of these jobs are on-campus and pay at least minimum wage, usually higher. To see if your student qualifies for this type of aid, again, complete the FAFSA process.

Once you've submitted your FAFSA, you'll receive a Student Aid Report, or SAR. Your SAR contains the information reported on your FAFSA and usually includes your Expected Family Contribution (EFC). The EFC is a measure of your family's financial strength and is used to determine your eligibility for federal student aid. The school(s) you list on your FAFSA will get your SAR data electronically. Each school will send you an award letter outlining the amount and types of financial aid – from all sources – the school is offering you. You can compare award letters from all the schools to which your teenager applies and make an informed decision.

Scholarships:

A **scholarship** is sum of money or other aid granted to a student, because of good grades, test scores, athletic skill, artistic skill, leadership qualities, and many other reasons, including just writing a great essay about why you want to pursue your education! You do not have to repay this money. Another opportunity for FREE money!

While there are many college-based scholarships that can be very generous, relatively few students qualify for them. There are, however, *many* scholarships available from local and national organizations. These organizations are actively searching for applicants! Awards can range from a few hundred dollars to a few thousand and if your student applies to several, the dollars can add up. Encourage your teenager to apply for scholarships no matter your financial situation, because financial need isn't always the most important criteria. Some ideas:

1. Search the Web. One idea: Go to www. scholarships.org and search their large database for a variety of scholarships.

2. Check with the career or counseling center at your high school. They often will have the names of organizations that offer scholarships and the applications. There are so many small scholarships from $100 - $1,000 that organizations are just dying to give away, but few teenagers apply. Those dollars can really add up. It's definitely worth a try.

3. Inquire at your place of employment about any scholarship programs available. Have your teenager do the same if they are currently working.

4. If you or your teenager belongs to any organizations, ask someone who works there if scholarships are available.

5. Talk to friends, neighbors, relatives about their employers and organizational affiliations.

Student Loans:

A **student loan** is a contract between you and the lender – usually a bank or the government. The lender agrees to lend you the money you need for tuition and other costs and you promise to pay the money back over time with interest. **Interest** is the cost of borrowing money expressed as a percent, such as 8.5%. Familiarize yourselves with some of the most common Federal Government student loans:

1. **Federal Perkins Loans:**
   These loans are available through schools for students in financial need. The US government loans the money to the school which passes it on to students. These loans are attractive because of their low interest rate – 5%. The maximum amount awarded depends on your financial status but can amount to thousands of dollars per year. You must be a U.S. citizen, national, permanent resident, or have other special status.

   Some advantages of Perkins Loans:
   - No credit check needed
   - Flexible repayment options
   - No prepayment penalty
   - A fixed 5% interest rate
   - Interest is subsidized while you're in school

To apply for a Perkins Loan, complete the Free Application For Federal Student Aid process - also known as FAFSA - as early as possible. For more information you may contact the Financial Aid office of any college or go to The Department of Education's website: studentaid.ed.gov.

2. **Stafford Loans:**

These loans are similar in many ways to the Perkins Loans with some exceptions. Two main differences are 1. a higher interest rate: 5.6% - 6.8%, and 2. Lower loan amounts available. Stafford Loans are, however, a bit easier to receive than Perkins Loans and you do not necessarily need to demonstrate financial need.   There are two types of Stafford Loans and if you demonstrate financial need, you will receive a lower interest rate than if you do not. Again, go to studentaid.ed.gov for more details.

3. **PLUS Loans:**

These loans allow parents (not students) to borrow very large dollar amounts so that all costs may be covered. The amount loaned is calculated after all other Federal Aid you are eligible for is determined. These loans are very different than the two above.

Here are some differences:

- Parents must pass a credit check
- You may pay a fee of up to 4%
- A fixed 7.9 – 8.5%% interest rate
- Interest will not be subsidized
- Repayment begins 60 days after the loan is made

There are many other details of all the above Federal Government student loans so be sure to check out the Department of Education website: studentaid.ed.gov.

There are also student loans available through every state. Go to your state's website and search under "Education" for details.

There are also student loans available through many **commercial banks**. If you have a high credit score, the interest rates are competitive with Federal loans. If you have a low credit score, you will pay more in interest.   The repayment timeframes and restrictions vary.   Check your own bank and other banks to compare rates and programs. Suggestion: Go to www.bankrate.com and look under "College Finance" for a variety of loans and rates.

***Step #3: The Brutal Reality
of Loans & Interest
Teach your teenager how a loan works –
in this case, a student loan***

If you and your teenager apply for any type of student loan, it is critical that both of you understand how a loan works and the amount of money that will be repaid on a monthly basis and in total. The media is full of stories about college students who graduate with a mountain of debt having no idea how to manage it. If your teen knows how loans work and they are realistic about future earnings, then they have a good chance of successfully managing their after-college debt .

Look at the two following charts:

MONTHLY PAYMENTS FOR STUDENTS LOANS

Chart assumes pay-back period of 15 years (except for Perkins Loan)

Type of Loan	Loan of $20,000	Loan of $50,000	Loan of $100,00
Perkins Loan @ 5.0% interest (Can borrow up to $27,500 if eligible. Must repay in 10 years)	$212 per month	N/A	N/A
Stafford Loan @ 6.8% interest (Can borrow up to $27,500 if eligible. Must repay in 10 – 25 years)	$178 per month	N/A	N/A
PLUS Loan @ 8.5% (Must repay in 10 – 25 years. Can't have bad credit)	$197 per month	$492 per month	$985 per month
Commercial Bank Loan @ 3.75% (With good credit. Must repay in 10 – 15 years)	$148 per month	$370 per month	$740 per month

Note: There are many details and restrictions that apply to the loans in this chart. The monthly payment amounts are estimates made using published interest rates at the time of this publication.

Will your teenager (or you) be able to handle a monthly payment for 15 years for the amounts estimated in the chart above? Obviously, much of that depends on the income your college graduate (or you) is earning when it comes time to repay.

In Chapter 4, *Where's Your Passion?,* You and you teenager spent time looking at the earnings potential of different careers. Go back and take another look at the starting pay and median annual pay for those careers. Take the starting pay and divide by 13. That number is a rough estimate of what your teen might earn each month.

Example: $35,000 ÷ 13 = $2,700 approximately. We use 13 rather than 12 (months) to account for taxes*.

Now look back at the chart.   How realistic will it be for your college graduate to make the payment that best fits your teenager's projected loan needs?

But a monthly payment isn't the end of the loan story. It's important for you and your teenager to understand the TOTAL loan amount that will be repaid over the course of the loan; in this case, 15 years.

*This is a quick way to provide a reasonable estimate. In Chapter 9, we will give you more accurate instruction on how to teach your teenager about estimating taxes using tax tables provided by the IRS.

TOTAL LOAN AMOUNTS PAID

Chart assumes pay-back period of 15 years (except for Perkins Loan)

Type of Loan	Loan of $20,000	Loan of $50,000	Loan of $100,00
Perkins Loan @ 5.0% interest (Must repay in 10 years)	$25,456	NA	NA
Stafford Loan @ 6.8% interest	$32,040	NA	NA
PLUS Loan @ 8.5%	$35,460	$88,560	$177,300
Commercial Bank Loan @ 3.75%	$26,671	$66,677	$133,354

Be sure that your teenager understands that, say for a Stafford Loan of $20,000, he or she will end up paying $32,040 when all monthly payments for 15 years are added together. That's because of interest; the cost of the loan. In this case, the cost of the $20,000 Stafford Loan is $12,040. The amount borrowed AND the interest paid plus any other money or aid he or she receives throughout college IS the true cost of education. It's very important that your teenager begin to understand that concept and how interest adds significantly to that cost. This may be your teenager's first lesson in how a loan – any kind of loan – works and why interest can be dangerous.

How can interest be avoided? Well, if you're going to take out a loan, it can't. But, there are several ways to pay LESS in interest over the course of the loan.

Both you and your teenager should know that interest paid on a student loan is tax deductible every year that you are paying off the loan.

DOLLARS & $ENSE

In 1997 Doug left the small town in Ohio where he grew up to attend the University of Southern California. Tuition was approximately $20,000 per year (and has since grown to $41,000 in 2010). Doug qualified for some grant money but didn't apply for any scholarships. Doug's major was undeclared for two years but he was interested in a degree in film and TV.

As a junior, however, he decided to major in Communications. By this time his grant money had run out and so had his parents' savings. To cover the last two years of school, he and his family took out loans. For spending money, Doug participated in the work-study program. He worked between 10 – 15 hours per week as an 'escort service'; driving students to and from campus to their apartments, as well as a cameraman videotaping professors teaching in the classroom.

During his time at USC, Doug enjoyed the highly diverse student body, so different from where he grew up. Doug also joined a fraternity and was an active participant. "As president of my fraternity, I learned a lot about leadership and having to deal with the administration of the school," on things ranging from fund-raising to out-of-control parties.

Doug graduated in 2001 with a degree in Communications unsure about his next steps. After several months of unemployment, Doug's parents suggested he look into teaching. Doug had a friend who recently graduated with a business degree and was really enjoying teaching math in middle school. After some research, Doug decided to enroll in a teaching credential program at California State University, Northridge. Doug borrowed an additional $3,000 to complete the two-year program.

It's 2011. Doug is 31 and a high school social sciences teacher who loves what he does. His parents have two more years of making payments for one of his undergraduate loans and Doug will finish paying off another of his undergraduate loans this year.

Doug admits that while he enjoyed his time at USC, he has never really taken advantage of the famous USC network. He is confident that he could have received an equal education at a much less expensive college and therefore saved himself and his parents years of loan payments. "I'd like to get my masters in history but I can't afford any more loans right now," he said recently.

Doug also says that despite the long-lasting financial implications of attending an expensive school like USC, he doesn't regret his decision to go there. He has come to appreciate the well-rounded college experience he received. "The one thing I should have done differently," Doug offers, "is I should have applied for more scholarships before and during my college years."

Step #4: How to Lessen the Pain
Discuss with your teen some ideas for
paying less interest on a loan

1. Make bigger payments than the required amount (check with your lender first to see if that's allowed). You will pay off the loan quicker and therefore pay less in interest.

2. If you receive a bonus at your job or some windfall of money, pay off the entire loan and avoid any more interest payments. (Again, check with your lender first to see if that's allowed with no penalty).

3. Get a part-time job while in college rather than taking out a loan or taking out as much of a loan.

4. Take a year before going to college, work your buns off and save like crazy. A loan might not even be necessary, or a much lower amount could be borrowed.

5. Find a less expensive college. We are always amazed at the number of parents we talk to who set no restrictions on applying to outra- geously expensive colleges in the first place. It is only after the teenager is accepted that the parent discourages their child from attending due to financial concerns. Is that really fair to the child? If you realistically analyzed the situ- ation and determine that you cannot or do not want to pay for a certain school for your child, don't let your teen apply!

Higher education has many advantages and often leads to better career opportunities. The impor- tant thing to remember is that once the education is through and the work begins, your young adult must be fully aware of his or her financial respon- sibilities and be able to meet those responsibilities successfully.

Step #5: Other Ideas About College and
College Planning
For-Profit vs. Non-Profit colleges

Over the past ten years, there has been much hype and controversy over the proliferation of for-profit colleges. Names like University of Phoenix, National, Corinthian and DeVry (for- profit institutions) are becoming as well known as Harvard and UCLA (non-profit institutions). For-profit colleges have experienced an enroll- ment increase of over 200%. Most students at- tend schools owned by one of the 15 large, pub- licly traded companies, places that enroll tens of thousands of students each year. While these col- leges offer an alternative path for students juggling work and family demands, it is important to un- derstand what you are receiving for your tuition and what might be lacking.

Focus on Accreditation

Accreditation determines a school's eligibility for participation in federal and state financial aid pro- grams. Both for-profit and non-profit institutions receive varying levels of participation in financial aid programs. However, proper accreditation is also important when it comes to acceptance and transfer of college credit during undergraduate as well as graduate programs.

Regional Accreditation

Generally, large well-known universities and statewide colleges (i.e., Harvard, University of Colorado), which are non-profit schools, are **regionally accredited institutions**. That means that these institutions undergo a voluntary and independent review of their educational programs in order to ensure consistency and sound quality. The most recognized and accepted type of accreditation in the U.S. is regional accreditation. **As a result, college credits or degrees awarded at a regionally accredited institution are often accepted by other regionally accredited colleges or universities. However, acceptance is not guaranteed. Each institution establishes its own policies based on their own programs. Non-regionally accredited program are not as accepted.**

There are six geographic regions of the U.S. with an agency that accredits colleges and university higher education programs. They are:

1. The Middle States Association of Colleges and Schools. This region includes Delaware, District of Columbia, Maryland, New Jersey, New York, Pennsylvania, and Puerto Rico.

2. The New England Association of Schools and Colleges. This region includes Connecticut, Maine, Massachusetts, New Hampshire, Rhode Island, and Vermont.

3. The North Central Association of Colleges and Schools. This region includes Arkansas, Arizona, Colorado, Iowa, Illinois, Indiana, Kansas, Michigan, Minnesota, Missouri, North Dakota, Nebraska, Ohio, Oklahoma, New Mexico, South Dakota, Wisconsin, West Virginia, and Wyoming.

4. The Northwest Association of Schools and Colleges. This region includes Alaska, Idaho, Utah, Montana, Nevada, Oregon, and Washington.

5. The Southern Association of Colleges and Schools. This region includes Alabama, Florida, Georgia, Kentucky, Louisiana, Mississippi, North Carolina, South Carolina, Tennessee, Texas, and Virginia.

6. The Western Association of Schools and Colleges. This region includes California, Hawaii, Guam, American Samoa, Commonwealth of the Marianas, the Marshall Islands, the Federated States of Micronesia, and the American/International Schools in East Asia and the Pacific.

Note: To be sure whether or not a college or university is regionally accredited and by which agency, visit the websites of the agencies listed above and look up the name of the institution.

National Accreditation

For-profit colleges and some smaller, private colleges are often accredited by national groups. Historically, for-profit colleges often focus on short-term college programs in fields such as medical billing, culinary arts and business administration. The U.S. Department of Education (www.ed.gov) and the Council for Higher Education Accreditation (www.chea.org) maintain directories of nationally recognized and specialized accrediting agencies. **Programs that are nationally accredited may not transfer to a regionally accredited institution.** Again, this may be critical to your college student if they wish to transfer and/or attend graduate school in the future.

Other Types of College Accreditation

Programs of study that are regulated by national or state licensing boards may require specialized or professional accreditation such as the National Council for Accreditation of Teacher Education and the American Bar Association. Again, check the directories of The U.S. Department of Education (www.ed.gov, search on accreditation) and the Council for Higher Education Accreditation (www.chea.org) if appropriate for your student.

Be sure you understand what accreditation your teenager's potential school is offering. **When it comes to for-profit vs. non-profit institutions, not all degrees are created equal.** This is important. Your teen faces a competitive job market and may need to transfer to a non-profit school or apply to a non-profit graduate school in the future.

College Admissions Coaches

There is growing trend where families employ a college coach to help navigate the entire college process, from preparation to application. The cost of these coaches may range from a few hundred dollars for helping with an essay, to $40,000 for crafting an entire strategy of getting your teenager into a prestigious school. While most parents love the idea of spending less time helping

their teens with college preparation and applications, consider the message you are sending to your child and what you both may be missing from taking on the experience together. Although time consuming, applying to colleges can be a rewarding experience and one that draws you closer as a family. And if your teen 'owns' the process, they will reap the consequences of their actions.

We do recognize, however, that there may be a place for a college admission coach. We recommend using a college coach in the following instances:

- **Neither parent has the time to devote to many hours of planning and research**. Planning for college, researching colleges, and applying to colleges takes numerous hours on the part of the parent as well as the student. It cannot be accomplished in a weekend or even over a few weekends. Patty Garfield, one of the authors, calculates that she and her husband spent over 300 combined hours on their daughter's journey from high school to college. Over a two year timeframe the parents and the teen visited a number of college campuses, were involved in on-going online research, evaluated various schools, and dealt with standardized testing, applications, meeting with school counselors, attending college fairs, and the list goes on and on. The whole process evolved as new ideas about majors, schools, finances, and careers required more thought and research. The hours added up quickly. If you are unable to devote this kind of time and genuine interest in the process, a college coach may be helpful.

- **You and your teenager do not get along well in situations where you have to spend a lot of time together, make compromises, come to agreements, and meet timetables**. As teachers and parents of teenagers, we understand that the teenage years are often very difficult ones for the parent-child relationship. The college application process should not be filled with tension and stress every single moment. To be sure, it's not stress-free, but it's also a time where you can learn, grow, and respect each other under relatively peaceful terms. We encourage everyone to be involved in the process at some level from the beginning. But if it proves extremely unpleasant for either party, a college admissions coach may be a godsend.

- **If your teenager or you are particularly weak in certain areas**. Terrible with time management? A horrible writer? Not adept at using a computer? Never been to college yourself? Don't let these weaknesses sabotage your teenager's chances of getting into a college that may be well suited for them. Honestly evaluate yours and your teen's weaknesses and if you can't tap other resources to make up the differences, a college admissions coach may help to fill the void.

If you are thinking of using a college admissions coach, get plenty of recommendations and ask to see the coach's results upfront. Then verify those results. Admittedly, there is a place for a college admissions coach's services for some families, just be certain you are using one for the right reason.

Free Informational Sessions

If you're a parent with younger children and trying to plan ahead, consider taking one of the many free seminars or informational sessions from investment advisory firms such as Fidelity. Ask your bank or credit union if they offer such sessions. Also inquire at work. Many employers will host informational sessions given by investment firms that handle your firm's 401k and pension programs.

Summary of Useful Websites

Website	Organization	Content
Studentaid.ed.gov	Department of Education	This website is your one-stop resource for everything you will need to learn about federal grants, loans and work study programs. It tells you how and when to apply, provides forms, talks about repayment options and offers a loan calculator. It also gives many good ideas on how to prepare and apply for colleges.
Fafsa.ed.gov	Department of Education	Direct link to the Free Application for Student Aid – part of the Studentaid.ed.gov website.
Nces.ed.gov	Department of Education	Data and statistics pertaining to colleges in the U.S. including college costs.
Collegeboard.com	The College Board (not-for-profit organization)	This website is arguably an essential resource in the college preparation/admissions process. The site offers a vast database of college information by school. Test preparation and registration information are provided. Information on how to pay for college along with loan calculators. Creators of Scholastic Aptitude Test (SAT) and sponsor of the Advanced Placement Exams (AP Exams).
Scholarships.com	Scholarships.com	Free database and search engine which uses a personal profile to identify the scholarships that are most relevant to each student. Uses a detailed questionnaire then generates a list of grants and scholarships available from state, local and colleges.
Fastweb.org	Fastweb	Free resource for paying and preparing for college.
Going2college.org	Mapping Your Future, Inc.	Teenager friendly site to explore career options, plan for college and locate financial aid sources.
Todaysmilitary.com	U.S. Department of Defense	Military scholarships website.
Ncaa.org	National Collegiate Athletic Association	Sports scholarships website
Health.gwu.edu	The HEATH Resource Center - a national clearinghouse on post-secondary education for individuals with disabilities. Managed by The George Washington University Graduate School of Education and Human Resources	Students with disabilities website

Website	Organization	Content
Uncf.org	United Negro College Fund, Inc.	African American scholarships website
Apiasf.org	The Asian & Pacific Islander American Scholarship Fund	Asian American scholarships website
Hsf.net	Hispanic Scholarship Fund	Latino scholarship websites
Latinocollegedol-lars.org	The Tomas Rivera Policy Institute	
Hispanicfund.org	Hispanic College Fund	
Maldef.org	Mexican American Legal Defense and Educational Fund	
Bie.edu	Bureau of Indian Education	Native American scholarships websites
Collegefund.org	American Indian College Fund	
Aises.org	American Indian Science and Engineering Society	
www.bankrate.com	Bankrate, Inc.	A great website loaded with all kinds of loan calculators including student loan calculators. Gives interest rate information on various loans. Provides lots of good information about saving and planning for college
Your state's website	State government	Visit your own state's website and check out the information under Education. All states offer student loan programs of their own.
www.ed.gov www.chea.org	The U.S. Depart-ment of Education (www.ed.gov) and the Council for Higher Educa-tion Accreditation (www.chea.org)	Accreditation information for many colleges and universities

Chapter Five Checklist:

Check off the items you and your teenager have completed:

☐ 1. Review your teen's career preferences and earning potential.

☐ 2. Teach your teen the differences between grants, work study, scholarships, and student loans.

☐ 3. Teach your teen how a loan works and how interest impacts the total amount owed.

☐ 4. Discuss some ways to reduce the amount of interest that is repaid.

☐ 5. Ask your teenager and LISTEN to them about what they are seeking from the college experience. Is it only a degree? Social activities and opportunities? Specialized training for a particular career? An opportunity to experience something different from 'home'? Or some combination of all these things? Separate in your mind what your teen is telling you from your own aspirations for them.

☐ 6. Have a realistic conversation about how much you as a parent are willing to finance of your child's education. Make a plan as to how together you might finance your teen's education.

☐ 7. Review the chart listing various websites and check out a few - together!

☐ 8. Map out your next steps together. Create a calendar with college visits, test prep classes, college application deadlines and grant deadlines all highlighted.

Notes

Chapter 6
THE SKY IS NOT THE LIMIT:
Budget and Plan

"Money isn't everything but it sure keeps you in touch with your children."

- J. Paul Getty

THE SKY IS NOT THE LIMIT:
Budget
& Plan

GOAL: To have teens learn how to budget and then plan for college or technical school and living expenses.

For many students and their parents, college is a big hurdle to clear. For students, the challenges are mostly academic, while for parents the challenges are largely financial.   It seems like a blessing to be able to send your teen away to college and not have him or her worry about tuition or expenses. But is it? Data suggests that college students are often unprepared (some would say clueless) about managing money and are unaware of differences between grants and loans and actual college costs. In fact, college is the time that many young people get into credit card debt because nobody ever took the time to explain the seriousness of credit cards and how to properly use them.

According to a study released in 2009 by Sallie Mae, the overwhelming majority of undergraduates across the nation owned a credit card in 2008, and the average card balance was more than $3,000. But even worse, many college students graduate with enormous debt burden just as their adult life starts to unfold. According to a report by the Project on Student Debt, students who graduated from college in 2010 with student loans owed an average of $25,250.

Can you afford not to educate your teen about their finances and the importance of a budget before they "leave the nest"? Are you confident they know how to manage money wisely, even when nobody is watching over their shoulder? Before your teen begins the next chapter in their life, we feel it's critical that you introduce them to the concept of budgeting. This should be a shared conversation where you both learn together. Who knows, you may find some great new solutions to keeping the cost of daily life down, down, down!

In this chapter we'll start with baby steps. What does a "budget' actually mean? How does it relate to a teenager? Can your teen create a budget for their monthly spending right now?   We'll take a look at the kinds of spending teenagers have these days and help them create and follow a budget while still in high school.

Budgets take on even greater importance in your teen's life after high school. Whether they head straight to university or technical school or combine work with part-time schooling, teens need a strong understanding of their income and their expenses to make the next few years work in their favor. Here is where budgeting becomes a planning tool. You and your teen will map out that first year of post high school life for each one of your teen's possible school choices. Identifying the expenses associated with schools of interest and then matching those costs with actual and potential sources of income will create Year 1 budgeting tools that both of you can use to help your teen navigate toward the right school.

To help, we've included 'snapshots' of several students who have set up budgets to get them through Year 1. Our students are a diverse group and their responses to the financial demands of education reflect their (and their parents') ingenuity and desire to make realistic choices that will help them achieve their goals. When it comes to budgets, there is no 'one size fits all.' It's about having clear goals, understanding true costs and balancing value against desire.

After completing the Year 1 budget, you and your teen can now project what four/five more years of schooling might cost.   Admittedly, this will be a very 'soft' number. Future college costs can be hard to project to the penny and there

may be unanticipated future events that can cause the most well thought-out budget to be revised. Even so, evaluating the total bill and possible total indebtedness at this point is extremely important. It helps you get a clearer picture of your newly minted graduate's potential future debt burden. With that information, you and your teen can make a final connection – which college or technical school choice results in manageable debt that your teen can handle given their estimated post college/tech school salary?

Step #1: Budget Basics

Alright, let's start with a clear definition. A **budget** is a sum of money set aside for use in the future. *The idea of a budget is proactive*, i.e. done in advance. Your teen may think it is the total spent **after** all the bills and incidentals expenses are added up. They need to learn the difference. We feel it is really important for your teen to learn to live within a budget, especially before they move away from home and are on their own. The approach your teen takes when studying for a big exam or writing a big paper also works when it comes to budgeting your money. You have to think and plan ahead to increase your odds of success.

Too many teens think budgets are financial prisons, but really they are just road maps and like every trip you take, you need to choose the best route. Budgets help you make choices. Thoughtful ones.

First, let's imagine life as a pie and our expenses as the slices. What do we typically spend our money on? The pie slices below make sense to adults who manage household expenses. A teenager's perspective is quite a bit different, so we encourage parents to discuss these slices with their teens so that they begin to understand how the expenses in your household add up.

Now have your teen create their own pie. Using a pencil, your teenager should divide up the pie into slices that estimate his/her spending. Have them write in a category for each slice. For reference, we've provided a list of typical categories teens spend money on.

EXAMPLE BUDGET

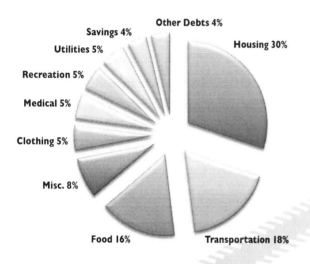

Other Debts 4%
Savings 4%
Utilities 5%
Recreation 5%
Medical 5%
Clothing 5%
Misc. 8%
Food 16%
Housing 30%
Transportation 18%

Source: VISA

MY PIE

As a parent there is often the guilt that you should be giving and providing, but sometimes the providing is NOT in the form of payment. Sometimes the giving is in the form of teaching and helping your children learn how to take care of themselves.

TYPICAL SPENDING CATEGORIES
FOR TEENAGERS

- Snacks
- School Activities
- Eating Out
- School Supplies
- Make Up
- Clothing
- Gas
- Entertainment
- Hobbies
- Car Payments
- Insurance
- Bus/Subway Passes
- Community/Church Donations
- Savings

What does your teen's pie look like? Are there any surprises? There may be adjustments depending on geography; for example, you may live where transportation or other costs are higher than the national average. A good question to ask now is whether your teen is pleased with how their pie is sliced.   Is their spending is in line with their wants and needs? For example, if you spend $100 a week on fast food, yet never feel very satisfied, should you continue spending money that way? Perhaps you would rather shop at the grocery store and cook at home most of the time, while going out for a great meal once a week.   Same cost, higher satisfaction.

DOLLARS & $ENSE

During the first week of class, the students were given a form to track their personal spending habits for two weeks. Anytime they used cash or a debit card for any kind of purchase, they were supposed to save the receipt and then record the amounts in class each day.

Maya noticed that most of her purchases were for food. She spent approximately $10 per day on food items: Starbuck's drinks, Flaming Hot Cheetos, Red Bull, and Sour Patch candy. This amounted to approximately $70 per week. Doing some quick math in her head she realized she was spending roughly $280 per month on food. She whipped out her calculator, and exclaimed, "OMG, that's $3,360 a year on junk food! That's disgusting!"

Maya asked others seated around her what their totals looked like. She was somewhat comforted to find that the story was similar among her peers. But Maya continued to think about her new revelation.

Then the students were instructed to give up at least one purchase per week and put the unspent money into their bank account for the entire semester. They also had to set a goal for how much money they would save and what the money would be used for at the end of the semester. Maya's goal was to save $20 per week which would amount to approximately $400 by the end of the semester. Feeling pretty happy with herself, Maya told the class, "I'm going to use that money for Christmas gifts."

The next day Maya came into class and immediately showed everyone that she had brought food with her from home. "I talked to my mom about all the money I was spending on snacks and she agreed to make me a healthy sandwich every day for the entire semester."

Every day, someone in the class would ask, "What kind of sandwich do you have today?" Maya would unwrap the sandwich and give us a report. On any given day, kids would look at the sandwich and say, "Wow that looks bomb! I want one of those." Maya would just smile and sink her teeth into it. Then, with a full mouth announce, "It IS the bomb!"

Toward the end of the semester, everyone had to give an update on the goal they set back in the fall. Maya was beaming when it was her turn to report, "I saved around $500 — more than my goal. I'm going Christmas shopping AND I'll have enough money to buy myself a venti-triple one-quarter pump sugar-free vanilla non-fat extra hot latte while I'm shopping."

Step #2: What's Your Burn Rate?

Remember your teen's pie was just an estimate. Now let's see what the real numbers look like.

A great exercise we use in our classes is for students to track their personal income and spending for one week. Afterward, the typical student response is astonishment. You would think they discovered the world is round! They never think about their cash flow patterns and they're amazed at how much they spend on food, gas, clothes and make-up. They also don't think about what it takes to earn money – especially if they automatically receive an allowance or get simple handouts from their parents – so they don't have a good understanding of their 'income' pattern either.

Activity:
Track Your Income and Spending

For the Teen
We suggest that you save your shopping receipts in an envelope for every purchase you make with cash or a debit card each day for one week. Use a piece of paper to record any other spending and any money received by parents or friends. Keep that in the envelope as well.

For the Adult
We suggest that you save your shopping receipts in an envelope for every purchase you make with cash or a debit card each day for one week. This is great modeling for your teen since you're asking them to do the same. Don't worry about checks, credit card purchases and other charges without

---

NEEDS vs. WANTS

receipts – the objective is to become more aware of cash and debit card usage on a daily basis. As for income, take your most recent paycheck amount and divide by the number of weeks it covers to get a weekly figure you can use for this activity.

Wrap-Up
At the end of one week, you and your teen should sit down together, turn to page 92, and take turns filling in the amount of money each of you received and spent during that week on the forms provided.

Try very hard not to condemn each other for your spending habits. While neither of you may approve of the way each spends money, this activity is about awareness, not about judgment.

As you fill in your chart notice that some expenses are **fixed** – that means that those expenses are the same each month and cannot really be adjusted by your spending habits. Most of the expenses are **variable** – that means that those expenses can be radically adjusted by the spending choices you make each day.

INCOME & SPENDING RECORD

Key: F = Fixed Expenses, V = Variable Expenses

FOR TEEN Record of Income & Spending One Week		FOR ADULT Record of Income & Spending One Week	
Income		**Income**	
Wages, Salary, Allowance, Borrowed $, Gift $, Other		Wages, Salary, Allowance, Borrowed $, Gift $, Other	
Total Income		**Total Income**	

Spending		**Spending**	
Saving – v		Saving – v	
Food/Dining – v		Food/Dining – v	
Clothing – v		Clothing – v	
Phone (cell & land) – f		Phone (cell & land) – f (Be sure to include the cell phone amount - even though the bill is monthly. Break it down to a weekly number for your teen.)	
Personal Services – v		Personal Services – v	
Auto Expenses/Transit – f		Auto Expenses/Transit – f	
Entertainment – v		Entertainment – v	
Gifts – v		Gifts – v	
Self Improvement –v		Self Improvement –v	
Charitable Donation - v		Charitable Donation - v	
Miscellaneous –v		Miscellaneous –v	
Total Spending		**Total Spending**	

Calculate the totals in each row and column. Once you are finished, both of you can see how much each of you earned and spent by category and in total. Fill in the answers below.

TEEN SUMMARY:

1. I received a total of $_____.

2. From _____ to _____I spent $_____.

3. My top 3 spending categories are

    _____, _____, & _____.

4. How do I feel about my spending choices?

5. What changes can I make to my variable expenses?

ADULT SUMMARY:

1. I received a total of $_____.

2. From _____ to _____I spent $_____.

3. My top 3 spending categories are

    _____, _____, & _____.

4. How do I feel about my spending choices?

5. What changes can I make to my variable expenses?

Once you and your teen have reviewed your income and spending patterns, it's time to talk about setting a monthly spending budget. Remember, a budget is a sum of money allocated for a particular purpose. Discuss whether or not your teenager should simply use their weekly burn-rate pattern and multiply by four (weeks in one month) to arrive at a monthly budget. Your goal is to agree on acceptable amounts and for your teen to stick to those – that's REALLY what a budget is. Go back to the Record of Income and Spending form and pencil in your teen's new, monthly numbers. This is their 'official' monthly budget. Everyone needs to learn how to set a budget and stick to it. It can be one of the hardest things to do when you start looking at your spending and your finances. We think it takes a little practice to get it right.

Step #3:
Look Around and Learn From Others

Now that your teenager has some idea of what a simple budget looks like, planning for that first year of college will make more sense and it will be easier for them to establish a reasonable budget for themselves after they leave the nest. But before you and your teen start to build a budget, let's stop and look at how some other families have built their budgets.

In the charts that follow, we have provided a look into the freshman year of different college students, a kind of snapshot with some important details. Point out to your teenager that each of these budget snapshots illustrates the interplay of two opposite events: expenses (or outflows of money) and income/sources of funding (inflows of money). By looking at these charts you will find out if these students received a scholarship or any type of financial aid or loans, how much debt they will have at the end of their first year, and how their family has set up their spending money. It's important to remember that financing education is often about accessing lots of different pots of money – savings, scholarships, grants, loans, work study, outside jobs, gifts, allowances, even the value of Advanced Placement classes and community college classes that translate into college credit. Each of the student snapshots detail the multiple sources they tapped to create a workable budget. Each student's situation is distinct with different backgrounds and socioeconomic levels.

Read through each one including the students comments and our own. Do you see any students who have a similar financial profile to your teen's? Following these charts, you'll find a blank snapshot for your teen to complete their Year 1 budget, adding in expenses and income/sources of funding. Remember, each family's snapshot is unique. There is no absolute right or wrong here. Still, we do think there are some strategies that are wiser than others and we hope to guide you along the way.

Note: In these snapshots, the term "Allowance" refers to money each teenager is given by parents or other family members to use for Living Expenses/Incidentals. The numbers from the Burn Rate exercise may help your teenager and you calculate the "Allowance."

SNAPSHOT #1: *LIVING ON CAMPUS BUT STILL CLOSE TO HOME*

Ashot - University of California, Irvine College Major: Math with plans to attend law school	

EXPENSES:

Tuition	$13.122
Room and Board	$11,611
Books	$1000 new & used
Other School Fees	Included in tuition
Transportation	*Car:* Drives family used car *Car Insurance:* Parents pay for car insurance *Car Maintenance:* Parents cover & Ashot still gets the good student discount.
Cell Phone	Parents pay for the bill and Ashot is still part of the Family Plan.
Living Expenses/ Incidentals	Clothes, gasoline, snacks, toiletries, going out, miscellaneous necessities paid for by parents & grandparents via Allowance
Debit Card	Got during junior year of high school.
Credit Card	Got while in high school. In his name – uses for all expenses & pays off each month.
Debt to Repay After Year One	$4,000

INCOME/SOURCES OF FUNDS:

Grants, Scholar-ships, Loans	Cal Grants, UC Grants, Scholarships, and Loans.
Work Study Program	On-campus work available through Financial Aid. Ashot does qualify to get this sort of work but is waiting out his freshman year and focusing on school.
Part-time Job (Other than Work Study)	None at this time – his parents have said that school is his job.
Allowance Setup	$300/mo from grandparents $100/mo from parents for gas Allowance is deposited into his checking account on the 3rd of every month. He uses his credit card during the month as needed paying close attention to spending then pays the bill off with his allowance. He has an ATM card to the account.
College Credits Earned While Still in High School	Ashot earned 51.5 college credits while still in high school by completing community college classes & by earning AP credit

Ashot's Comments & Advice: "The only person who can stop you from achieving anything is yourself. Take as many college classes as you can while you are still in high school. The tuition is usually free and it can make a huge difference when you actually get to college. I just finished up my first real quarter at UC Irvine, but I'm already considered a sophomore. That will make a huge difference in terms of final cost!"

Author's Comments: Ashot worked hard through high school taking college level courses. This could conceivably help him finish his undergraduate studies in a little over three years instead of the typical four and it translates into savings of approximately $20,000. It's remarkable that Ashot didn't have to work at a job for that money, but simply made school his 'work'. Make sure that you and your teen are looking at courses in high school that could potentially be applied toward an undergraduate degree.

SNAPSHOT #2: *LIVING ON CAMPUS AND WORKING DURING THE YEAR*

Stephanie - Yale University College Major: English	

EXPENSES:

Tuition	$40,500
Room and Board	$12,200
Books	$600 new & used
Other School Fees	Included in tuition
Transportation	N/A
Cell Phone	Parents pay for the bill and Stephanie is still part of the Family Plan.
Living Expenses/ Incidentals	Clothes, snacks, toiletries, going out, miscellaneous necessities paid for by Stephanie and parents via Allowance
Debit Card	Got during junior year of high school and had issues with overdrafts and fees.
Credit Card	Issues with debit card have kept her from getting a credit card at this time.
Debt to Repay After Year One	$0

INCOME/SOURCES OF FUNDS:

Grants, Scholar- ships, Loans	92% funded through Financial Aid The balance was paid by the family funds saved for college. No loans were taken.
Work Study Program	N/A
Part-time Job (Other than Work Study)	Had a part-time job on and off during the year and worked at a law firm during the summer after freshman year to save up spending money for sophomore year.
Allowance Setup	No set allowance but family helps as needed.
College Credits Earned While Still in High School	No college credit earned

Stephanie's Comments & Advice: "Students should take advantage of a part-time job, even if they feel as if they don't have the time for it. Because often the jobs on campus will pay a higher hourly rate and it's worth your time. Also set up some sort of investment savings plan so that any money they do have set aside can be earning money while they are in college."

Author's Comments: Stephanie is an excellent example of a student who receives financial assistance largely on academic merit. The trends in college aid do favor students whose excellent academic performance makes them attractive to recruit and retain. Even so, Stephanie knows that the next few years may require her to fund 8-10% of her education and she is prepared to meet her financial needs via work study or part-time jobs, and if necessary, loans.   Parents should explore the ways in which their college bound teens can work part-time either on or off campus or in a work/study position through the financial aid office.

SNAPSHOT #3: *FAR AWAY FROM HOME, NO DEBT*

Michelle - Tulane University College Major: Communications	
EXPENSES:	
Tuition	$43,434
Room and Board	$11,450
Books	$1,100 new & used
Other School Fees	Included in tuition
Transportation	*Air Travel:* Approx. $1,800/year to fly round trip to and from Los Angeles
Cell Phone	Parents pay for the bill and Michelle is still part of the Family Plan.
Living Expenses/ Incidentals	Clothes, snacks, toiletries, going out, miscellaneous necessities paid for by both Michelle and parents via Allowance.
Debit Card	Has debit card with her checking account.
Credit Card	Parents co-signed – for emergencies only
Debt to Repay After Year One	$0

INCOME/SOURCES OF FUNDS:

Grants, Scholar-ships, Loans	100% funded by parents. No loans were used.
Work Study Program	N/A
Part-time Job (Other than Work Study)	Worked summer job before college and saved to use as spending money.
Allowance Setup	Receives approx. $80/mo from parents.
College Credits Earned While Still in High School	1 Advanced Placement Test

Michelle's Comments & Advice: "I lived my whole life in California but decided to go away to Tulane in Louisiana. It was an adjustment but has been a great decision. Don't let the fact that the school is close or far from home influence your decision."

Authors' Comments: Michelle's parents have largely shouldered the burden of college. As a result, Michelle may not have a real appreciation of the costs of her decision to attend Tulane or what hardship her parents are bearing as a result of her decision. In fact we feel that the distance of a school from home should be a real financial consideration, part of the positives and negatives when evaluating your teen's college acceptances.   Was Tulane by far the best educational opportunity for her? What did Tulane offer that she couldn't find closer to home?

P.S. We followed up with Michelle's parents who said indeed these issues were part of the family's decision making and that they concluded Tulane was still a great choice.

SNAPSHOT #4: *LARGE DEBT AT THE END OF YEAR ONE*

Chelsea - School of Visual Arts in New York City Major: Photography	
EXPENSES:	
Tuition	$29,550
Room and Board	$22,800
Books	$830 new & used
Other School Fees	Included in tuition
Transportation	N/A
Cell Phone	Parents pay for the bill and Chelsea is still part of the Family Plan.
Living Expenses/ Incidentals	Clothes, gasoline, snacks, toiletries, going out, miscellaneous necessities paid for by parents & grandparents via Allowance
Debit Card	Has debit card with her checking account.
Credit Card	Parents co-signed – for emergencies only
Debt to Repay After Year One	$0 for Chelsea. Parents refinanced home to finance Year 1 of college.
INCOME/SOURCES OF FUNDS:	
Grants, Scholar- ships, Loans	50% funded by scholarship from school. 50% funded by parents
Work Study Program	N/A
Part-time Job (Other than Work Study)	None
Allowance Setup	Receives approx. $300/mo from parents transferred to checking account.
College Credits Earned While Still in High School	Although Chelsea took a few AP classes in high school, her new school doesn't accept them for credit.

Side Note: Chelsea's mother is primarily a homemaker and her father was a successful contractor until 2008 when his business took a major hit in the recession. To date the family is getting by on their savings and refinancing their home. They intend to use refinancing funds to pay for Chelsea's first year at school.

Author's Comments: The recession of 2008 hit families hard throughout the country but especially those families with businesses tied to real estate. While Chelsea's parents want to fulfill their daughter's dream, it might come at too high a cost right now. We don't think it's ever wise to liquidate retirement and savings accounts to pay for college.   While your teen has a lifetime of earnings ahead of them, you as parents have a shorter time frame to "re-earn" your liquidated savings. Also unclear is how the family will pay for years two through four. There should have been a serious examination of other options, including a less expensive school or putting college off a year so the teen could work and save. It's hard to say no to your child, but sometimes a more financially manageable approach ends up being better for everyone in the long run.

DOLLARS & $ENSE

John comes from an entrepreneurial family; his mom and dad own a successful tile business and invest in distressed real estate. John worked part-time jobs throughout high school, from vitamin store sales person to selling and stocking tile at the family business. So it was no surprise that when John got to college – University of Arizona – he was looking for a business opportunity that would be exciting and potentially lucrative.

Wasting no time during his first semester, John and his friends noticed that most students stayed up late studying, taking food breaks throughout the evening. All of them agreed that fresh baked cookies and milk seemed like a natural combination and they saw virtually no competition. 'Hot Box Delivery' was born in the kitchen of a small apartment offering homemade chocolate chip, sugar, and peanut butter chocolate chip cookies and milk. For $5.00 a student could have freshly baked cookies and a quarter gallon of milk delivered right to their dorm or apartment by "hot girls" who were decked out in a company uniform, designed by one of the founders.

Hot Box Delivery was well received by the coeds of Tucson and the guys made money even after plowing back most of the profit into the business. But after one year, the guys all joined a fraternity and their 'free time' became less free. But John doesn't regret the experience, "We had fun creating the business and watching it grow. I learned that persistence is one of the keys to success."

After the cookie business folded, John moved on to various jobs at the Marriott Hotel in Tucson. But getting his foot in the door wasn't easy. "I applied five times before I finally got my first job there. One day I just walked in and basically demanded an interview. I asked to speak to a manager and I told him I just wanted 5 minutes. The interview turned into a much longer meeting and I wound up working in the gift shop. My advice to teenagers is to take whatever job is available and be good at it. Take pride in what you learn and what you earn. Working keeps you organized and boosts your confidence."

What has John done with most of his earnings? Besides using it for spending money, John has traveled; twice to Europe and twice to Mexico. Recently, John has been looking at real estate deals in and around the Tucson area and hopes to invest in rental properties with his dad.

Not every family can afford to send their teen away to college nor does every teen have the grades or desire to go straight to a four-year school right after high school. Whatever the reason, some teens choose to stay close to home and commute to school or attend the local community college. Here are a few different snapshots of college freshman who live at home. Some attend full-time, some part-time, some work, some don't. Most are expected to pay for part of their expenses or help out with the family bills. We know that every family relationship is a little different, but here are a few that we feel are quite typical.

SNAPSHOT #5: *SMART SELF-STARTER NEEDS CASH*

Luther - Loyola Marymount University Major: Communications	

EXPENSES:

Tuition	$36,500
Room and Board	N/A (lives at home, doesn't pay rent)
Books	$500 rented online
Other School Fees	Included in tuition
Transportation	*Car:* Luther makes monthly payment *Car Insurance:* Luther's mom pays for it *Car Maintenance:* He covers most all small repairs / mom helps if there is a big repair
Cell Phone	Luther pays his own cell bill.
Living Expenses/ Incidentals	Clothes, snacks, toiletries, going out, miscellaneous necessities paid by Luther.
Debit Card	Has had debit card since he was 17.
Credit Card	Got the credit card when he got his debit card at 17. Credit limit continues to increase and he pays off card each month.
Debt to Repay After Year One	$10,000

INCOME/SOURCES OF FUNDS:

Grants, Scholar- ships, Loans	$15,000 grant from LMU $11,500 in Federal and school loans
Work Study Program	This was offered to Luther but he turned it down to work on his own business – LA Clique (clothing design).
Part-time Job (Other than Work Study)	Various office jobs and DJ-ing in clubs until he started his own clothing design business.
Allowance Setup	$0 – mom out of work for 2 years.
College Credits Earned While Still in High School	Luther earned 3 college credits by taking a college class through a free program provided by Woodbury University.

Luther's Comments & Advice: "Get involved in high school socially and again in college – it really sets the tone. 'Learn' the professor AND the material. Pay attention to the details. Apply to many colleges – don't just play it safe."

Author's Comments: Luther has a lot going for him. He takes his studies seriously and has a clear entrepreneurial spirit. Luther knows that he'll need to watch every dollar between now and graduation, but understands that education can make his business dream a reality. We suggest that Luther look at costs and benefits: How much time does he spend each week nurturing his own business? What if he worked for someone else? Could that help reduce his total college debt, (on par to reach $40,000 or more when he gets that degree)?

SNAPSHOT #6: *WORK WITH SCHOOL ON THE SIDE*

Troy - Santa Monica College College Major: Business	

EXPENSES:

Tuition	$1,000 - Troy goes to school at night part-time.
Room and Board	N/A (lives at home, doesn't pay rent)
Books	Approx. $400
Other School Fees	Included in tuition
Transportation	*Car:* Troy pays 20% of payment, Dad pays the rest *Car Insurance:* Troy's dad pays for it *Car Maintenance:* He covers most all small repairs / dad helps if there is a big repair
Cell Phone	Troy pays $25 per mo., dad pays the rest
Living Expenses/ Incidentals	Clothes, snacks, toiletries, going out, miscellaneous necessities paid by Troy.
Debit Card	Has had debit card since he was 16.
Credit Card	Got the credit card when he got his debit card at 16. Credit limit is $300 and he tries to pay it off in full every month.
Debt to Repay After Year One	$0

INCOME/SOURCES OF FUNDS:

Grants, Scholar- ships, Loans	$0
Work Study Program	N/A
Part-time Job (Other than Work Study)	Troy began working part-time as an unpaid intern which later turned into a full time paid position.
Allowance Setup	$0
College Credits Earned While Still in High School	Troy earned 6 college credits by taking a college class through a free program provided by Woodbury University and by taking another class at a community college.

Troy's Comments & Advice: "Save your money. Think hard before you spend your money on a big purchase. These are important years – what you do now dictates where you will be in 10 years. Try new things. Be adventurous. Meet new people. Network. Never be scared of the word no...keep trying!"

Author's Comments: Troy is like many young people who start working and try to get their under-graduate degrees via night school. At 8 credits a semester it will take a while before Troy is able to transfer to a four year school, either full or part-time. So our advice to Troy is – bank your salary from the PR job. That may help you take a work break and finish up your degree full time without incurring a lot of debt. Remember that your degree will translate into higher earnings and you'll be a more competitive job candidate once you've graduated.

SNAPSHOT #7: *SWEAT THE SMALL STUFF*

Erica - California State University, Northridge College Major: Business Administration	

EXPENSES:

Tuition	$4,800
Room and Board	N/A (lives at home, doesn't pay rent)
Books	Approx. $1000
Other School Fees	Included in tuition
Transportation	*Car:* Erica's parents bought her a car before school started. *Car Insurance:* Parents pay for it. *Car Maintenance:* Parents pay for maintenance.
Cell Phone	Parents pay for the bill and Erica is still part of the Family Plan.
Living Expenses/ Incidentals	Clothes, snacks, toiletries, going out, miscellaneous necessities paid by Erica.
Debit Card	Has had debit card since she was 16.
Credit Card	Got the credit card before starting college – to be used for emergencies.
Debt to Repay After Year One	$0

INCOME/SOURCES OF FUNDS:

Grants, Scholarships, Loans	$0
Work Study Program	N/A
Part-time Job (Other than Work Study)	Erica works part-time as a hostess and waitress approx. 25 hours/week.
Allowance Setup	$0
College Credits Earned While Still in High School	Erica earned 9 college credits by taking one college class through a free program provided by Woodbury University and by passing two Advanced Placement Tests.

Erica's Comments & Advice: "Be mindful of all you do. Careful with your spending and academics. Don't let freedom push you over the limit. When you go to college you don't seem to have any limits anymore and that's scary and can get you into trouble! Pay attention to your credit score – it helped me a lot when I went to rent my first apartment."

Author's Comments: Erica is in great shape with all the big issues covered. She can stay at Cal State Northridge for her entire college career and has solid financial support from her parents. So, it's time to sweat the small stuff. Erica needs to keep her spending under control, be prompt in paying her bills, keep the credit card hidden away and not let little 'splurges' add up. She needs to pay attention to her credit score and save as much of her part-time job earnings as possible. That will all come in handy when she needs to apply for other credit such as loans, utilities, and credit cards.

SNAPSHOT #8: *CHANGES AHEAD*

Sarkis - Los Angeles Valley College & Glendale Community College College Major: Finance	

EXPENSES:

Tuition	$2,500
Room and Board	N/A (lives at home, doesn't pay rent)
Books	Approx. $1000
Other School Fees	Included in tuition
Transportation	*Car:* Sarkis received a car from parents as a high school graduation gift. He does not make payments. *Car Insurance:* Sarkis pays for 80%, parents cover the rest. *Car Maintenance:* Sarkis pays for 80%, parents cover the rest if needed.
Cell Phone	Sarkis pays his share of bill - he is still part of the Family Plan.
Living Expenses/ Incidentals	Clothes, snacks, toiletries, going out, miscellaneous necessities paid by Sarkis.
Debit Card	Has had debit card since he was 16.
Credit Card	Got the credit card before starting college and pays it off every month.
Debt to Repay After Year One	$2,500

INCOME/SOURCES OF FUNDS:

Grants, Scholar-ships, Loans	Receives Federal Financial Aid
Work Study Program	N/A
Part-time Job (Other than Work Study)	Sarkis has his own music production business. He creates music and sells to artists and singers.
Allowance Setup	$0
College Credits Earned While Still in High School	Sarkis earned 29 college credits by taking many classes at local community colleges.

Sarkis' Comments & Advice: "I would highly recommend high school students to start taking college classes during their junior year. It is a great way to experience the college atmosphere and you will gradu-ate from college a year earlier than your classmates. As a full-time student, you should never settle for the regular 13 units. I found myself having too much free time on my hands when I did, so after that my minimum became 16 units and I still had plenty of time to study."

Author's Comments: Sarkis is a classic transfer student. He did well academically in high school, has a lot of college credits already under his belt. However, he will need to find a four year school soon in order to complete an undergraduate degree. While he hasn't incurred a lot of debt yet for education, he hasn't earned much yet at his part-time job. Our advice is that Sarkis get a part-time job that pays more and save most of that money in preparation for the cost of finishing up his degree. He needs to watch his expenses and be savvy when it comes to choosing his next school. Read the following *Dollars and $ense* story to see what happened to Sarkis.

DOLLARS & $ENSE

Sarkis has played piano since he was a little kid. In high school he became curious about how to add other instruments to his piano playing and so he started learning about computer software that allowed him to do just that. In time, he discovered 'beats' — the non-vocal layer of the song not including instrumentals, which is frequently based on a looped recording of a drum-rhythm — commonly heard in rap and hip hop music.

After playing some of his beats for his friends, Sarkis was encouraged to perfect his new found interest. One day in weight training class, Sarkis approached a rapper and told him about his beats. The guy was so impressed, he paid Sarkis $100 for one of his pieces.

After two years of junior college, Sarkis transferred to California State University at Northridge. While completing his 4 year degree in business, Sarkis created a YouTube page where he posted his music in the hopes that other rappers would take notice. They did, and Sarkis was able to raise his prices providing a steady stream of income. In fact, former NBA All-Star, Steve Francis, saw Sarkis' YouTube page and now he and Sarkis are working together on producing music.

And that's not the only way Sarkis makes money while attending California State University at Northridge. Sarkis buys used text books from Amazon and then sells them online at two strategic times; either right after finals (when most students don't bother to take the time to sell them) or within two weeks of the start of school (when students who have procrastinated become a bit desperate and will pay higher prices).

Finally, Sarkis has a part-time job with Chase bank and is studying for his real estate license. According to Sarkis, "It's not hard going to school and working and making money. You just have to be disciplined and organized."

Step #4: Complete the Year 1 Snapshot

Now it's time for your teen to complete snapshots for every school they are serious about. **Begin by using the expenses for various colleges your teenager researched on page 69 to fill in your teens' snapshots: Tuition, room and board or meal plan, fees, and books.**

Next, look back at your teen's Burn Rate Activity on page 93. Let's refine those numbers as much as possible. Will your teen's spending pattern during Year 1 of college include all those same expenses? (Remember that the Burn Rate Activity expenses reflect weekly expenses. Make sure that your teenager calculates expenses for a full school year. It takes a little multiplication to forecast those over the typical nine month academic year, and if your teen will be living away from home, they'll have some additional expenses to consider, like weekly groceries, transportation for visits back home, etc.). Focus in on some of the small details first. Is a car really a necessity and if so, who is going to pay for insurance, maintenance and gas? What about the cell phone plan? Can a cheaper, but less comprehensive plan suffice? What about clothing? School supplies? Books? Are there ways to economize?

Now let's look at the income side. Brainstorm together about how the student can limit college debt via work study, part-time jobs, or by researching and applying for scholarships. Remind them that they are expected to pay for some of their own college expenses, especially monthly living expenses or some book costs.

Some parents mandate that their child put a small amount of money away in savings from each paycheck. This will help them learn the value of savings as well as help them build a small nest egg when the time comes to move out.

YOUR SNAPSHOT: FRESHMAN YEAR (Use data from page 69 & page 93)

SCHOOL A - YEAR I	
EXPENSES:	
Tuition	
Room and Board	
Books	
Other School Fees	
Transportation	
Cell Phone	
Living Expenses/ Incidentals	
Debit Card	
Credit Card	
Debt to Repay After Year One	

INCOME/SOURCES OF FUNDS:

Grants, Scholar- ships, Loans	
Work Study Program	
Part-time Job (Other than Work Study)	
Allowance	
College Credits Earned While Still in High School	

SCHOOL B - YEAR I	
EXPENSES:	
Tuition	
Room and Board	
Books	
Other School Fees	
Transportation	
Cell Phone	
Living Expenses/ Incidentals	
Debit Card	
Credit Card	
Debt to Repay After Year One	

INCOME/SOURCES OF FUNDS:

Grants, Scholar- ships, Loans	
Work Study Program	
Part-time Job (Other than Work Study)	
Allowance	
College Credits Earned While Still in High School	

YOUR SNAPSHOT: FRESHMAN YEAR (Use data from page 69 & page 93)

SCHOOL C - YEAR 1	
EXPENSES:	

Tuition	
Room and Board	
Books	
Other School Fees	
Transportation	
Cell Phone	
Living Expenses/ Incidentals	
Debit Card	
Credit Card	
Debt to Repay After Year One	

INCOME/SOURCES OF FUNDS:

Grants, Scholar- ships, Loans	
Work Study Program	
Part-time Job (Other than Work Study)	
Allowance	
College Credits Earned While Still in High School	

SCHOOL D - YEAR 1	
EXPENSES:	

Tuition	
Room and Board	
Books	
Other School Fees	
Transportation	
Cell Phone	
Living Expenses/ Incidentals	
Debit Card	
Credit Card	
Debt to Repay After Year One	

INCOME/SOURCES OF FUNDS:

Grants, Scholar- ships, Loans	
Work Study Program	
Part-time Job (Other than Work Study)	
Allowance	
College Credits Earned While Still in High School	

Step #5: Translate that Snapshot into a Monthly Budget

Now that you and your teen have thought about annual college expenses, set up a monthly budget. Have your teen take the numbers from their snapshot and divide by the number of months they will be at college during the year – typically 9 months. Use these monthly figures to help fill in the Monthly Budget Form we have provided on the next page. You may have to estimate expenses in some cases.

The Monthly Budget Form looks similar to the Record of Income and Spending in the earlier Burn Rate Activity, but this time you and your teenager are actually planning ahead, not just recording past activity – you are budgeting! *And by the way, the total income numbers and total expense numbers should match.*

Note: We realize that some income and expenses are not received or paid monthly, e.g. tuition, room and board, fees, books, student loans. This budget is meant to reflect only those items that your teenager will be dealing with monthly.

> **Think about how your snapshot will look in year 2, 3, 4...**

MONTHLY BUDGET: College Year 1

INCOME	School A
Grant, Scholarship, Loan	
Wages (Work Study & Part-Time Jobs)	
Allowance	
Other	
Total Income	

EXPENSES	School A
Food/Dining – v	
Clothing – v	
Rent – f	
Electricity – f	
Heating/AC (gas) – f	
Water & Sewage – f	
Phone (cell & land) – f	
Personal Services – v	
Car/Transit Expenses – f or v	
Home Furnishings – v	
Entertainment – v	
TV Cable/Dish – f	
Internet – f	
School Supplies – f	
Gifts – v	
Self Improvement –v	
Saving – f	
Charitable Donation - v	
Miscellaneous –v	
Total Expenses	

MONTHLY BUDGET: *College Year 1*

INCOME	School B	School C	School D
Grant, Scholarship, Loan			
Wages (Work Study & Part-Time Jobs)			
Allowance			
Other			
Total Income			

EXPENSES	School B	School C	School D
Food/Dining – v			
Clothing – v			
Rent – f			
Electricity – f			
Heating/AC (gas) – f			
Water & Sewage – f			
Phone (cell & land) – f			
Personal Services – v			
Car/Transit Expenses – f or v			
Home Furnishings – v			
Entertainment – v			
TV Cable/Dish – f			
Internet – f			
School Supplies – f			
Gifts – v			
Self Improvement –v			
Saving – f			
Charitable Donation - v			
Miscellaneous –v			
Total Expenses			

Step #6: The Big Picture - Projecting Costs Over Four Years

You and your teen have done a lot of work creating Year 1 budget snapshots and detailed monthly budgets for your teen's prospective schools. Placing those various snapshots side by side should give you both a clearer picture of the financial challenges of each school choice. Now it's time to consider that college and technical school lasts for several years. So let's take those numbers and expand them over the total numbers of years you think it may take for your teenager to complete their education. Decide if your family can sustain these school costs all the way through. Now it's time to get an idea about what the total 'bill' might look like after 4 or 5 years of college or technical school.

Activity:
What's the Grand Total?

Fill in the chart below:

COLLEGE OR TECHNICAL SCHOOL COSTS FOR ALL YEARS

		School A	School B	School C	School D	Page Reference
1.	Tuition x # years expected to attend school					Pages 106 & 107
2.	Fees and books per year x # years expected to attend school					Pages 106 & 107
3.	Average yearly spending x # of years expected to attend school					Use monthly expenses from pages 108 & 109 and convert to yearly number.
4.	TOTAL EDUCATION COSTS ALL YEARS (Add rows #1-3)					N/A
5.	Estimated debt to be repaid x # of years expected to attend school					Pages 106 & 107

Have an honest conversation that may include the following:

- Is it realistic to assume that you both are able to stick to this budget and pay for it?

- Which costs are likely to rise?

- How can you both contribute more money if necessary?

- What steps can you take now to ensure that there will be enough money to pay for the college/technical school years?

As your teenager begins college/technical school or a hybrid of college/technical school and work be sure to review the year one snapshot and monthly budget you developed together. See how accurate you were at predicting expenses and income. You may have to adjust your budget as conditions change but always have yearly and monthly plans you and your teen can review at least twice a year. Helping your teenager with this process throughout their education will instill a discipline of monitoring their cash flow for life. They will be more likely to become financially responsible and avoid some of the dangers of living paycheck to paycheck.

> ### Debt & earning potential are critical in college decisions.

Step #7: The Financial Forecast

When it comes to their son's or daughter's life after high school, most parents are concerned about one thing. We call it the **FINANCIAL FORECAST**. Stated as a question it looks like this:

Will my child be able to support themselves working at a job they enjoy and one that has future potential?

With all the research you and your teen have done so far, it's time to make an educated stab at answering that question. You have both collected lots of important data, like what careers your teen is considering, what kind of education does he or she need to start a career, what schools might be the best place for their education, what are the costs associated with various schools and what kind of money can your teen expect to earn upon graduation. All the pieces are here. Now it's time to plug them in and finish your forecast.

The following chart in this chapter is the final one for you and your teenager to complete. But remember, the purpose of this culminating activity is **not** to pigeon-hole your teenager or limit their opportunities or aspirations. Instead it is meant to revisit the question we asked in Chapter 4: "Where's Your Passion?" and now lay out a solid financial plan that recognizes your teen's passions, talents, skills and brains and leads them to a satisfying career with a future. Your teen has researched several possible careers of interest. Let's start with his or her top career choice. Fill in the Career Research section, rows #1-3.

	CAREER RESEARCH	Fill in this column	Page Reference
1.	Top career choice		Pages 56 & 57
2.	Education/training needed		Pages 56 & 57
3.	Estimated starting annual earnings		Pages 56 & 57

Now that your teen has filled in rows #1-3, have him/her plug in the financials for their top choice school in rows #4-5.

	EDUCATION RESEARCH & COSTS	Fill in this column	Page Reference
4.	Top school choice		Page 110
5.	Total education costs (all years combined)		Page 110, line #4

And now you, the parent, plug in the estimated income sources in rows #6-10.

	PAYING FOR EDUCATION	Fill in this column	Page Reference
6.	Parent contribution (all years combined)		Page 108
7.	Student contribution (all years combined)		Page 108
8.	Other family contribution (all years combined)		Page 108
9.	Amount of money that may be offered from grants and scholarships (estimate)		N/A
10.	Total debt to be repaid upon graduation (estimate)		N/A

Now you have a reasonable "guesstimate" of the amount of money your teen may owe upon graduation. That money must be repaid. You and your teen now must determine how that "debt burden" will alter the Financial Forecast Question: **"Will my teen be able to support themselves working at a job they enjoy and one that has future potential?"**

To support themselves young people must make enough money to pay for housing (usually rent) transportation, food, clothing, medical, entertainment, utilities (including phone) **and their monthly student loan bill**. Plus they need to be able to save and a little every month and make charitable donations from time to time. Let's build a new financial "pie" with this in mind. To help determine the size of your pie slices we've pulled average percentages from the pie on page 88. Also, your teen has already researched their starting salary and to get a rough estimate of a monthly paycheck, divide the total annual salary by thirteen (We add an extra month to account for taxes – a very rough estimate! In Chapter 9 we'll show you how to get a more realistic estimate).

The last expense you and your teen need to determine is the monthly student loan payment amount. Grab a computer and go to: bankrate.com (or any website with a loan calculator). At bankrate.com:

- click on College Finance
- click on Loan Calculator
- fill in Loan Amount, Loan Term, Interest Rate (there are tools on the web page to help you estimate), and Loan start date
- click Calculate and you'll get a monthly payment amount

Now plug the monthly payment amount into row #12. Your monthly paycheck amount goes into #11 and the rest of your expenses can be filled in rows #13-22.

YOUR TEEN'S STARTING OUT BUDGET POST COLLEGE/TECHNICAL SCHOOL

		Fill in this column	Page Reference
11.	Estimated Starting Monthly Earnings (take annual amount ÷13 to account for taxes)		Page 112
12.	Student Loan (use amount from loan calculator)		N/A
13.	Saving (row #11 x .10)		N/A
14.	Housing (row #11 x .30)		N/A

YOUR TEEN'S STARTING OUT BUDGET POST COLLEGE/TECHNICAL SCHOOL

		Fill in this column	Page Reference
15.	Transportation (row #11 x .18)		N/A
16.	Food (row #11 x .16)		N/A
17.	Clothing (row #11 x .05)		N/A
18.	Medical (row #11 x .05)		N/A
19.	Entertainment (row #11 x .05)		N/A
20.	Utilities (row #11 x .05)		N/A
21.	Charitable Donations (estimate)		Pages 108 & 109
22.	**TOTAL MONTHLY EXPENSES** (add row #12 thru #21)		N/A

Now, let's put in our last numbers. Subtract your teen's total monthly expenses in row #22 from his or her estimated monthly earnings in row #11.

Estimated Monthly Earnings
(row #11, page 113): _____

- Total Monthly Expenses
(row #22, page 114): _____

= _____

Are the earnings greater than your expenses (a positive number)? If yes, terrific! You and your teen have a Financial Forecast that makes sense. On the other hand, if monthly expenses are greater than monthly earnings (a negative number), your teen and you should consider the following:

- Evaluate the other possible school choices on your list and see if any of those meet your financial criteria. You and your teen might also want to spend some time looking at other schools which may not have made your 'top five' list but can also be considered as viable educational options.

- Encourage your teen to work with their high school counselor and search out more 'free' money – scholarships and grants – to go after. You as a parent may want to approach relatives for possible financial help which will keep the loan amount as small as possible.

- Consider a 'gap' year where your teen puts off school for a year to work and save money, thereby reducing the total amount that will need to be borrowed. Also your teen may want to consider a combination work and study approach that will lengthen the time to graduation but reduce the overall debt burden.

- Some combination of the above.

Remember: Even if this chart is never fully realized by your teenager (most college students change their majors and career goals at least once) you and your teenager have spent the time to think through some of life's most important financial decisions – and you've done it together. That's Time Worth Spending!

Chapter Six Checklist:

Check off the items you and your teenager have completed:

☐ 1. Review budget basics and complete the Burn Rate Activity.

☐ 2. Review all college student snapshots.

☐ 3. Fill in their own snapshot for their top college choices.

☐ 4. Discuss and set a monthly budget for freshman year.

☐ 5. Fill in the College or Technical School Costs For All Years chart to project total school costs, then discuss whether or not these numbers are affordable.

☐ 6. Complete the Financial Forecast chart.

☐ 7. Review your teen's snapshot and monthly budget every year.

Notes

SECTION III

Chapter 7
CARRY A TOOLKIT:
Career Readiness Essentials

"By failing to prepare you are preparing to fail."

— Benjamin Franklin

CARRY A TOOLKIT:
Career Readiness Essentials

GOAL: To have teens prepare themselves for job interviews and the workplace environment.

The students who work and/or volunteer throughout their high school and college experience are the ones who learn how to manage their money and time. So, it's important for teens to learn basic work-related etiquette, how to find a position and how to best function in the workplace.

Step #1: Get Your Paperwork Done

Now is a great time to have your teen create a resume, reference page, and cover letter. Your teenager may be looking for a job or volunteer position and they may be asked to include a resume in a college or scholarship application. These documents do take time to create and

finalize so it's better to start now. Your teen can have all their paperwork at the ready to meet any opportunities that arise.

We have found that this activity in our classroom is one of the most fun and rewarding for the students. Our students tell us over and over how impressed most potential employers are when presented with professional looking documents from a teenager. Help your teenager fill in the provided forms to get started and then transfer it over to the computer. Remember, the Internet is loaded of great sites to help lead you through all of these steps including helpful templates. Your teen will have the leg up on so many other teens when they go out into the job market and search for their first job.

The Resume
Your teen's goal is to write up a one-page summary of their qualifications that potential employers will

read and be interested enough to want to have them back for the interview. This is their time to sell themselves. If they can't tell someone why they are the best person for the job then how can they expect someone to be interested in hiring them? Of course, they need to be careful with writing and typing. Your teen's resume can't have any spelling or grammar mistakes. If their potential employer finds typos and errors they are going to wonder what kind of work your teenager can produce for them under the time pressures of the workplace.

We suggest resumes be written in the present tense even when referring to past work and experiences. This helps reduce confusion for the reader. Also, avoid using the word "I" in a resume. All descriptions should be written in fragment sentences for brevity's sake. Be prepared to help as they create their first drafts.

Websites great for the resume, references and cover letter are:

theresumebuilder.com
freeresumesamples.org
exampleresumes.org

A word of caution: Make it clear to your teenager that they must tell the truth. *Never, ever lie or distort the truth in a resume.* If a potential employer discovers that your teen has taken liberties in presenting their qualifications or experiences, odds are your teen has ruined their chance at a job. Even worse, their reputation will be damaged and may prevent them from getting a job at other companies. Employers often share information among themselves.

Personal Contact Information: This information always goes at the top of a resume and must be accurate. Be sure to go over your address with your teen and how to write it properly. This is also the time to talk about their email address. It should be professional. Prettyprincess@yahoo.com just isn't going to cut it in the workplace. If they choose to list their cell phone as their primary contact phone number, have them decide if the ringback tone and voicemail message are appropriate. Also coach your teen on the professional way to answer the phone while they are on the job hunt. Have your teen fill in the info below:

Objective: This should be at most one or two sentences telling the potential employer what type of employment you seek. There are many example objectives on the Internet so start searching. Have your teen fill one in below:

Education: Your teen should highlight where they are currently attending school and any special classes they may have taken or are taking. Your teenager should only include their GPA if it is above a 3.0. List that information below:

Experience: Your teen should highlight any work or volunteer experience. If they have worked, they should include the company they worked for, their dates of employment, positions held, and a list of their duties. Tell them to choose their words wisely. Don't undersell. Now is not the time to be self-deprecating. Have your teen look online for a special list of ***action verbs*** to describe all of their duties. Suggested websites: resumetoolbox.com/action-verbs.html, resume-resource.com/resumeverbs.html. Have your teen fill in this information below:

Skills: Your teenager should list any special skills they have in this section. Again, don't undersell. Do they have a reasonable command of a second language? Can they fix computer problems? Are they skilled at caring for small children? Have your teen search online for a list of skills and see if they fit into any categories. Have your teen fill them in below:

Clubs & Activities: Your teen should list any clubs, sports, and activities they participate in. Be sure to note if they are a team captain or hold an officer position. Be careful to spell out club affiliations instead of using initials (i.e. Junior Achievement not JA). They can list them in bullet form and describe them if needed. Fill in below:

Honors & Awards: Your teenager should list any honors or awards they have earned in this section. Be careful that they don't go back too far in their past to find an award they earned. In addition to academic honors and awards, your teen should list any awards earned from a sport or a club too. Those awards are equally important and show a different side of your teen that might interest their potential employer. However, if they don't have any honors or awards don't include the section. Have your teen fill in below:

Example of a student resume:

Gary Andrews
535 York Drive
Burbank, CA 91505
(818) 555-5555
garyandrews@gmail.com

OBJECTIVE
Offering excellent computer, communicative, and analytical skills. Seeking to apply these skills to fulfill a position in an office environment.

EDUCATION
Burbank High School, Class of 2011, GPA 3.34
Honors and Advanced Placement Classes:
- Honors English, Biology and Chemistry
- Advanced Placement Classes: European History and US History
Specialized Coursework through the Academy of Finance: Accounting, Economics, Banking/Credit, Financial Services

WORK EXPERIENCE
Youth Services Worker, City Attorney's Office, Burbank, CA, June 2010 - August 2010
- File, copy and shred various legal documents

VOLUNTEER WORK HISTORY
Student Volunteer, Providence Saint Joseph Medical Center, Burbank, CA, 2010
- Maintain orderly patient files, assisted with general office duties
Literacy Tutor, Burbank Central Library, Burbank, CA, 2009-2010
- Assist elementary students with reading and writing
Drama Teacher's Assistant, John Muir Middle School, Burbank, CA, 2007
- Critique plays, construct stages

HONORS & AWARDS
History Student of the Year, Burbank High School 2008 - 2009
Industry Education Council Award for Economics, 2010
ROP Outstanding Student, 2009-2010
Junior Achievement Success Skills Certificate, 2009

EXTRACURRICULAR ACTIVITIES
Burbank High School Academy of Finance, Class Officer, 2009 - present
Math Club, Burbank High School, 2009 - present
National Honor Society Member, 2009 - present
Tennis Team, Burbank High School, 2007- 2008

REFERENCES
Excellent references available on request

DOLLARS & $ENSE

Greg is a Regional President of a national real estate services firm. He regularly speaks to our classes about his experiences interviewing and hiring people. He often tells the story about interviewing Derek, a seasoned professional who seemed to be the perfect candidate to handle Greg's regional marketing campaign. "Derek had a unique set of prior work experiences that set him apart from the other people I was interviewing. He had an engaging personality and everyone who met him in my office thought he'd fit in well. I personally checked his references and they were impeccable."

As a final step in the hiring process, the human relations department verified any potential employee's college credentials. "My HR person called me and to my dismay informed me that Derek never graduated from the college he listed on his resume. He simply lied."

Greg went on to explain that he found himself in an ethical dilemma. Here he had found an individual who seemed ideal in every way to fill an important position. Greg didn't even care about the college degree, "Frankly, his experience and personality were far more important to me than any degree Greg could have. I would have hired him without it. But the man misrepresented himself and I had to pay attention to that. What kind of message would it have sent to the rest of the people in my office if they found out I hired a person who did that? Also, if Greg misrepresented that information, what other things might he be hiding – now and in the future? His actions caused me not to trust him. I can't have people working for me I don't trust."

When Greg made the phone call to tell Derek that he didn't get the job and that his HR department discovered the truth about his resume, Derek was devastated. According to Greg, Derek begged him to overlook that mistake. Derek apologized and admitted what he had done was wrong. But Greg remained firm. Derek didn't get the job, a great job and one of very few available at that level at that time. It was 2008 and the Great Recession was in full swing.

The Reference Page

The reference page is a separate document presented to potential employers pursuing the next step in the hiring process. We don't recommend including references on the resume itself for two reasons: First, they take up a lot of space and a teenager's resume should be kept to one page. Secondly, It's not a good idea to have your reference contact information scattered all over town.

If a potential employer would like to hire your teen, they will ask for references and then it is appropriate for your teen to give them the reference page.

The top of the reference page has your teen's personal contact information and is formatted EXACTLY the same as the top of their resume. This is really a pretty simple document to create but the thought your teen should put into it may take time. A reference page should consist of a list of at least three people who can tell their potential employer about the teen's credibility, integrity, and work ethic. Do NOT list a family member or friend as a reference. Your teen must approach at least three and ask them if they could provide a "positive" reference, should they be asked. Your teenager should not assume that a good reference is automatic. It's always wise to check with the person and make sure.

Have your teenager start thinking about who they would like to use as their references. As a high school student, some great options are teachers, coaches, counselors, administrators, and club advisors. If your teen has some work experience or babysitting, pet sitting, house sitting, or volunteer work they should definitely use their direct supervisor. Remember they need to contact the reference first and ask for permission and then be sure and get the correct professional contact information for them. Have your teen look up the address and phone number online if applicable and then confirm it with them. Your teenager should always include the following information for each reference:

- Name
- Title
- Company
- Address
- Phone
- Email

Now it's time for your teenager to create their own reference page. Find the information for 3 references and fill in below:

Reference #1:

Reference #2:

Reference #3:

Example of a student reference page:

Gary Andrews
535 York Drive
Burbank, CA 91505
(818) 555-5555
garyandrews@gmail.com

Ms. April Martinez
Administrative Analyst II
Management Services Department
305 East Olive Avenue
Burbank, CA 91510
(818)555-5555 x305
amartinez@burbankcity.org

Ms. Caroline Samson
World History Teacher
Burbank High School
905 N. Third Street
Burbank, CA 91702
(818) 555-5555 x104
carolinesamson@burbankusd.org

Mr. Dave Black
U.S. History Teacher/Key Club Co-advisor
Burbank High School
905 N. Third Street
Burbank, CA 91702
(818) 555-5555 x105
daveblack@burbankusd.org

The Cover Letter

The cover letter is a must when mailing, faxing, emailing, or even dropping a resume off in person. It should always accompany a resume. Consider the cover letter as your teen's opportunity for a personal introduction. It will be the employer's first impression of your teen and we all know first impressions are important. The cover letter should be one page and have no spelling or grammatical mistakes. The cover letter gives your teen the opportunity to introduce themselves in a narrative fashion using sentence and paragraph format. It also gives the potential employer a first glimpse into their writing abilities. Be sure your teenager does some research and demonstrates that they understand a bit about what the company does.

There are a multitude of sample cover letters and tips on the Internet. Do a search for resume cover letters and check out all the available information. Be sure that your teen's personal contact information at the top of the cover letter looks EXACTLY like the top of the resume and reference page. Go straight to the computer and get started.

Be sure to encourage your teenager to let someone proof read the letter before it goes out. We find that our teenagers – even the straight A types – make many mistakes in spelling, punctuation, grammar, and capitalization. Once the letter is ready to be sent, your teen should sign it using blue or black ink. Help your teenager properly address an envelope, fold the letter in thirds, apply proper postage and mail it. This is a life-long skill that is critical for your teen to master.

Example of a student cover letter:

Gary Andrews
535 York Drive
Burbank, CA 91505
(818) 555-5555
garyandrews@gmail.com

July 30, 2010

Ms. April Martinez
Administrative Analyst II
Management Services Department
305 East Olive Avenue
Burbank, CA 91510

Dear Ms. Martinez,

My name is Gary Andrews, and I am currently a senior at Burbank High School. I am applying for the position of Youth Services Worker, which I heard about through your presentation in my Accounting class. I have enclosed my resume for you to review.

During my last three years of high school I have had worked hard at maintaining a 3.34 GPA. I am a Senior Officer of the Academy of Finance Program at my school. I enjoy tennis and mountain biking in my free time and I was on the Burbank High School tennis team in ninth grade. I am also a member of our school's Math Club and a member of the California Scholarship Federation. I have volunteered at John Muir Middle School where I helped my previous Drama teacher with his play, as well as at Providence Saint Joseph Medical Center. These clubs and activities have taught me management, communication, and computer skills. I feel that I can offer many things to the Youth Employment Program at the City of Burbank.

I would like to thank you for taking time out of your busy day to review my application. I would love to have the opportunity to participate in this learning experience. I am available anytime after 3:30 p. m., Monday through Friday. I look forward to hearing from you soon. Thank you again for your time.

Sincerely,

Gary Andrews

Step #2: Prepare For The Interview

Whether your teenager is interviewing for a job at McDonald's or for a highly competitive internship at the White House, there are some basic steps they should take to help ensure a successful interview.

Your teenager should:

- Research the prospective organization and the person who will interview them. Be knowledgeable about what the organization does, recent news events, and the key people in charge. Potential employers often ask, "What do you know about our company?" and "Why do you want to work here?" Doing a little research will help your teen answer those questions thoughtfully.

- Go online and search for interviewing questions. After checking a few sites your teenager will notice that there are roughly 10 standards questions that most employers will ask during an interview. Encourage your teen to develop concise answers to these questions before the interview.

- Develop a list of questions they would like to ask about the position and the company. Employers like to see that potential employees are curious and take initiative during the interview. Your teen should take that list with them in a professional looking notebook.

- Take a few extra copies of their resume to the interview. Your teenager may be meeting with more than one person and it will demonstrate their level of preparedness.

- Dress for success. For most interviews, it is appropriate to dress formally and conservatively even if that may not be the day-to-day attire of the organization. Your teen should convey an attitude of seriousness and professionalism, not have their clothes or body become a distraction.

  » *Girls:* Your teen should wear dark colored dress pants or a tailored skirt modest in length. A button up shirt or blouse that goes well with the outfit is appropriate. Cleavage should be covered up. Your teenager should keep jewelry and makeup to a minimum. If your teen has multiple piercings, she should remove them for the interview. Piercings should be limited to earlobes. Tattoos should be covered. Hair should be neat and pulled off the face. 1" – 3" heels are appropriate and should compliment the outfit – not create a focus point. Avoid strong perfume. Remember, if your teen is wearing anything that could also be worn to a party or club, help her find something else!

  » *Guys:* Your teen should wear dark colored dress slacks with a brown or black conservative belt. The color of the belt should match the color of the dress shoes – no sneakers or casual shoes. He should wear dark colored dress socks that fully cover his ankles when sitting down. Be sure your teen has a well pressed, button up collared shirt, preferably white or light blue accompanied by a well tied necktie that compliments the outfit. If your teenager doesn't know how to tie a tie, teach him how in advance of the day of the interview. We highly suggest your teen wear a plain, white undershirt as well.

DOLLARS & $ENSE

Linda is a Senior Vice President with a world renowned public relations firm. Linda spends over 50% of her day trying to convince decision makers in large companies to hire her company to handle their public relations issues. (Public relations are marketing efforts that influence the way the 'public' may view a particular company or organization such as TV news coverage.)

Linda's firm regularly hires college interns in an effort to hone and potentially hire new employees. Not long ago, Linda hired Haley, a new graduate from Northwestern University. Linda told us that once during an important presentation to a conservative potential client she noticed a rather prominent tattoo on Haley's ankle. The young woman had only been working at the PR firm a few months and mostly wore pants so Linda had never noticed the tattoo before. "I was horrified that Haley would think it was alright to participate in a meeting with a tattoo showing. We had been working on this client for months and we were being considered in the final cut of PR firms. I couldn't help but think the tattoo would cost us the business."

After the presentation Linda had a difficult talk with Haley. She explained that in certain situations and with certain age groups tattoos are often offensive and therefore, could be detrimental to the PR firm and to Haley's career. Linda went on to say that Haley had two choices: she would have to wear pants with hosiery in any future presentation with potential clients or she would have to get the tattoo removed. Haley was embarrassed and upset that her new boss felt it necessary to point out something so personal. But from that day on, Haley made sure she wore pants with appropriate hosiery to all presentations.

DOLLARS & $ENSE

Rebecca is a partner in a private equity firm who speaks to our students every year about workplace etiquette. (A private equity firm is a company that pools money from investors and then uses that money to invest in other companies that need funds to expand.) She tells a story of why dressing appropriately is critical to success in many careers. Rebecca explains that a few years ago she hired Elizabeth, a young woman, right out of Harvard Business School, who had all the talent, instincts, and ambition to be highly successful in a very competitive industry.

Every day Elizabeth would come to work with a different hairdo; sometimes it was pinned up with random pieces sprouting out, sometimes it was coiled around like small snakes atop her head, sometimes it was hanging down with a small section pinned back. The combinations seemed endless and often her sunglasses would be sitting on top her 'do' like a head band or tiara.

It didn't take long for others to notice and then begin gossiping about her 'dos.' Jokes were traded and wagers made between other office workers about how Elizabeth would wear her hair on any given day.

One day, after an important meeting with all of the firm's partners in which Elizabeth was asked to participate, Rebecca pulled Elizabeth aside. She told her that although she had the brains and smarts to make it in the private equity world, she wouldn't get very far given the way she presented herself. From conversations with the other partners Rebecca knew that they weren't taking Elizabeth very seriously and therefore, didn't give her work or opinions much consideration. Rebecca explained that while Elizabeth's peers might find her appearance acceptable, most older colleagues and clients would find it off putting.

"I realized that Elizabeth needed to be told. She simply didn't know better because no one had ever explained this to her before. Even though she had gone to an Ivy League school, even though she had had a prestigious internship, she just didn't understand that appearances matter a lot."

Facial hair should be well groomed or freshly shaved. Avoid heavy aftershave or cologne. Hair cut should be neat and clean. Jewelry should be kept to a minimum. We recommend that all piercings be removed, even in the ears. All tattoos should be covered.

- Arrive ten minutes early. This extra time will allow your teenager to gather their thoughts and look around the work place. Your teen will pick up a lot of information by noticing the people who work there and how they interact with each other. What does the environment feel like? Is it formal, serious, casual, hectic?

- Be very courteous to the receptionist and anyone who greets them. Any of these people may provide feedback to the 'boss.'

- Give a firm handshake and introduce yourself with confidence. Your teen should look the person they are interviewing with straight in the eye. Inform your teen that they should wait to be invited to sit down.

- Listen attentively. Let your teen know that they should answer questions thoughtfully, keeping their answers brief and to the point. It's OK to ask your interviewer to repeat the question if you don't understand. Never lie or make up answers to 'look good'.

- Ask questions but not too many – your teen is the one being interviewed, not the other way around.

- Smile!

- Finish strong. Tell your teenager that when the interview is over, thank the interviewer, shake their hand again and ask for a business card. The card will have all the contact information they may need in the future and it will come in handy when your teenager writes a thank you letter.

Example of a student thank you letter:

Gary Andrews
535 York Drive
Burbank, CA 91505
(818) 555-5555
garyandrews@gmail.com

August 15, 2010

Ms. April Martinez
Administrative Analyst II
City of Burbank
Management Services Department
305 East Olive Avenue
Burbank, CA 91510

Dear Ms. Martinez,

It was a pleasure meeting you and learning more about the Youth Services Worker program at the City of Burbank.

I feel confident that I have the proper qualifications to excel in the position you described. I have a strong work ethic and I am punctual. I learn quickly and I work well with many kinds of people. My knowledge of Microsoft Word, Excel, and PowerPoint would be a great asset to your organization. Furthermore, I possess the time management skills necessary to balance work and school successfully.

I remain very interested in the position and I feel certain that I could make a meaningful contribution to your organization. Thank you for your time and consideration. I look forward to hearing from you.

Sincerely,

Gary Andrews

Step #3: Write a Proper Thank You Letter

After the interview your teenager will breathe a sigh of relief – they made it! But let them know, they're not done. It is extremely important that your teenager understand how important it is to write a professional thank you letter within 24 hours after the interview.

The purpose of the thank you letter is three-fold:

1. To express appreciation to the interviewer for their time and consideration.

2. To confirm your teen's interest in the job and confirm that they are well qualified to fill the position.

3. To demonstrate your teen's ability to communicate effectively.

Most of the teens we teach do not know how to properly format a business thank you letter. Even though your teenager may be earning an A in an Honors English class, do not assume they use proper grammar, punctuation, spelling and capitalization. We recommend that somebody (not another teen though) proof read the letter before it is sent. We have provided an example letter for your teen's reference.

Once the letter has been typed and proofread, your teen should sign it using blue or black ink. Help your teenager properly address an envelope, fold the letter in thirds, apply proper postage and mail it within 24 hours. Your teenager may also deliver the letter in person – another opportunity to express interest and effort to the employer.

Step #4: Have The Facebook Talk - Now!

It is an important time to have a talk with your teen about Facebook or whatever social networking site they may be using at the moment. Many teens think they are invincible in many ways. Sure, they know deep down that they can get hurt and they have all heard the lectures, but that doesn't mean they don't push the envelope from time to time.

It would really be a shame for your teen to do all this research and find a job or internship, finish college and land a great career only to screw it up with a stupid mistake on Facebook. It has happened time and again. In fact there is an entire Facebook page dedicated to people who have been fired because of what they have posted on Facebook! From inappropriate pictures to poor choices of words to sharing of confidential patient information, people have lost their jobs after a few key strokes. Employers are increasingly using Facebook to vet potential job candidates. They look for status updates and photos to see what kind of person your teenager really is – outside of the workplace. Your teen can lose the job before they even get it.

Final Words

For most adults, much of what is recommended in this chapter seems like plain, old-fashioned, common sense. However, the teenagers we teach aren't born knowing these things and that holds true for your teenager as well. They can learn quickly, but they must be told and shown properly. Take the time to share these lessons with your teenager. Time spent now will help them get the jobs they need to become financially independent.

Chapter Seven Checklist:

Check off the items you and your teenager have completed:

☐ 1. Create a resume.

☐ 2. Create a reference page with three references.

☐ 3. Create a cover letter.

☐ 4. Discuss proper interviewing etiquette.

☐ 5. Review how to write a thank you letter after your teenager has an interview.

☐ 6. Discuss the importance of caution with social networking sites.

Notes

Chapter 8
HIT THE ROAD:
Cars and What They Cost

"Driving a brand new car feels like driving around in an open wallet with dollars flapping by your ears as they fly out the window."

- Grey Livingston

HIT THE ROAD:
Cars and What They Cost

GOAL: To have teens learn about the costs of operating, buying and leasing an automobile.

If your teenager is driving, chances are good that the costs of operating, buying or leasing an automobile are a mystery to them. Sure, many teens pay for gas, an occasional oil change, a car wash, and sometimes car insurance premiums. But let's face it, few parents have held teens accountable for all the costs involved in car ownership, mostly because we know that teens rarely have the income to pay for car related expenses. Still, for most teens, a car is in their near future and parents should take the time to educate them about the financial truths of that all-important set of wheels.

Cars have a way of sucking money out of your pockets with incredible frequency. Most experts will tell you that a car loses approximately 20% of its value the second we drive it off the lot. **In fact, most people spend more of their income on a car than on any other item except housing and food**. Unless you're buying a true collectible, cars only decrease in value over time. They are NOT an investment!

The next three steps will help your teen understand in detail the costs of owning a car. Then Step 4 and Step 5 will help you both consider the financial aspects of leasing or buying a car. Then it's time to put it all together in Steps 6-15 to figure out what your teen can afford, what financing they can potentially access and what kind of car matches their needs.

DOLLARS & $ENSE

For years Tito couldn't get his head above water; his expenses always exceeded his income. He'd pay most of his bills late and then receive late fees. Every month the bulk of his paycheck went toward old debts not to things he needed now. Eventually, he got so tired of that pattern he started spending his paycheck on having fun first and then whatever was left over, he'd grudgingly use to pay old bills. This only made him fall even further behind.

At the time, Tito was driving a KIA. He got two months behind on payments and tried to negotiate with the bank. They wouldn't budge. The bank proceeded to call him every day for months and eventually repossessed his car. To add insult to injury, the bank then sent Tito a bill for the loan balance. Tito spent months and years writing letters to try and clear his loan obligation. The stress of his entire financial situation caused him "to feel sick a lot of the time in those days."

With zero money saved and still living paycheck to paycheck, Tito took out a loan and bought a new VW Bug to replace the KIA. From the start, the new car had problems. Trying to cut corners, Tito would make the repairs himself but they never remedied the problems. Tito eventually sold the Bug at a loss – he still owed money on the loan.

The reality was Tito needed a car. Living in Los Angeles, a public transportation nightmare of a city, Tito needed to commute to his job and college campus daily. So Tito put his pride aside and bought a used car for $400 cash. To cover the old, fully exposed foam seats, Tito cut up and manually sewed old jeans for seat covers. "Fixing the seat covers was the beginning of fixing many things in my life," says Tito.

Slowly, very slowly, Tito began to change his behavior. He sought credit counseling from a non-profit organization. He took their advice. His credit score started to rise. He began to gain more respect for himself and his relationships with others improved. He stills drive the jean-machine with pride. Tito says, "I had to change my attitude about spending, about how I 'present' to others. Once I was able to let go of that mindset, things began to improve." It has taken eight long years for Tito to re-build himself and have those new behaviors 'stick.' As Tito explained, "There are things that are so difficult, so desperate, that only patience can get you through."

Step #1:   The Costs of Operating a Car

Whether your teen borrows a family car or has their own to drive, they should know the on-going costs of operating a car.

- **Gas**: Have your teen fill in the chart below with your help. Tell your teen how many miles each of your cars get per gallon and the number gallons each tank can hold. Have them multiply the current price of gas per gallon by the number of gallons per tank to determine the cost of a tank of gas.

CHANGE THE OIL!

The single most expensive component on any car is the engine. By changing the oil religiously every 3 months or 3,000 miles, whichever comes first, you will increase the life of your car's engine significantly. And just topping off the oil doesn't count!

FUEL COST COMPARISON

	Car #1	Car #2	Car #3
Miles per Gallon			
Gallons per Tank			
Current Price of Gasoline			
Price of a Full Tank of Gas (Price x # of Gallons)			

Compare the fuel efficiency of each car (miles per gallon) and why each car is different (size, use, type of gas). Some teens already know this information but for many, this is an eye-opener!

- **Registration, title, taxes and fees**: All states charge a fee to register a car title. A **title** is a legal document that establishes ownership. Show your teen a title to at least one of your cars. Point out who is the legal owner (usually the lender if there's a loan) and the registered owner (you). Explain that there are title fees and sales taxes only at the time you buy the car. However, you must pay a license tag fee each year and pay for emissions testing in most states every couple of years.

- **Maintenance and Repairs**: The owner's manual tells you what services your car needs and how often. Show your teenager the chart in the owner's manual that outlines the recommended maintenance schedule. Find any information you have about the cost of scheduled maintenance and share it with your teen. Tell your teen that they should also plan for unscheduled repairs such as flat tires, broken belts, dead batteries, and leaking hoses. Many of these repairs are costly and they will increase as the car ages. Locate any information you have about repairs related to your cars and share it with your teen.

- **Accessories**: For many teens, this may be the only sexy part of this lesson, so have some fun. How much do new rims cost? How about that spoiler, special paint job, or enhanced bass amp? Any added features will obviously cost money but impress upon your teen that not all add-ons will increase the value of the car. If you've spent money on anything from seat covers to extra alarm systems, share those costs with your teenager.

Now have your teenager fill in the chart below.

ADDITIONAL OPERATION COST COMPARISON

	Car #1	Car #2	Car #3
License Tag Fee			
Emissions Fee			
Maintenance			
Repairs			
Accessories			

At this point you may want to take a break before tackling the issue of car insurance. After all you don't want to throw too much at your teenager at once or they will tune out!

Step #2: Car Insurance – so boring, yet so important!

Of all the basic types of insurance, car insurance can be the most complicated. But if your teenager understands the fundamentals, they will be able to understand medical, life, homeowners and other types of insurance when those become necessary. Spend time now to get your teen familiar with the terms and concepts of insurance.

Insurance is a method for spreading individual risk among a large group of people to make losses more affordable for all. It provides relief from fear of severe financial loss due to events beyond our control.

An insurance company is known as the **insurer**. It agrees to pay the cost of potential future losses in exchange for regular payments by anyone who buys a **policy**. A policy is a legal contract between you (the **policyholder**) and the insurance company and the price of the policy is known as the **premium**.

Most states require minimum automobile insurance for registration of a motor vehicle. The premium for insurance coverage is expensive. Premiums are based on a number of factors such as:

1. Make, model, style, and age of the car
2. Driver classification (age, gender, marital status, driving record)
3. Location of driver and car (city, county)
4. Distances driven
5. Purpose of driving
6. Age and gender of other regular drivers of the car

Discounts are available for certain conditions such as good grades in high school and college and number of vehicles insured by the same company.

Your driving record includes infractions (traffic tickets), along with your accident record. An infraction may include a parking ticket, failure to come to a complete stop at a stop sign, or an improper turn. Speeding, driving without a license or driving recklessly are serious offenses called misdemeanors. Very serious offenses, such as drunk driving, hit and run, or leaving the scene of an accident, are called felonies. Felonies and misdemeanors increase your premiums and often result in loss of your license. Share with your teen any examples from your past that have increased your premiums.

There are five basic types of automobile insurance: liability, collision, comprehensive, personal injury protection (PIP), and uninsured/underinsured motorist.

Liability Coverage

Most states require all drivers to carry liability insurance.

*   *Purpose:* To protect the policyholder against claims for bodily injury to another person or damage to another person's property. It pays NOTHING toward the policyholder's own losses – either personal injury or damage to the vehicle. If the accident is not your fault, then the other driver's liability coverage pays for you. Liability coverage is described using a series of numbers such as 100/300/50. These numbers mean that the insurance company will pay up to $100,000 for injury to one person, $300,000 total for all people, and $50,000 for property damage in an accident. You may purchase higher coverage; however, the premium will be higher.

Collision Coverage

- *Purpose:* To protect your own car against damage from accidents in the event that you are at fault. Most collision insurance has a **deductible**. A deductible is a specified amount of a loss that the policyholder pays before the insurer is obligated to pay anything. The insurance company pays only the amount in excess of the deductible. YES, that's right – the policyholder pays premiums and then ALSO must pay a deductible before the insurance company will pay a cent. Our students are always outraged by this practice!

Comprehensive Coverage

- *Purpose:* Coverage for your car from damage from other causes like fire, theft, tornado, hail, water, falling objects, natural disasters, or acts of vandalism. Usually, there is no deductible (or a very small one) for comprehensive insurance.

Personal Injury Protection (PIP)

- *Purpose:* Insurance that pays for medical, hospital, and funeral costs of the policyholder and his or her family and passengers, regardless of fault. If you are injured as a pedestrian or bicyclist, this insurance will also pay for your medical costs.

Uninsured/Underinsured Motorist Coverage

- *Purpose:* To pay for your injuries when the other driver is at fault but has either no insurance or too little to cover the costs. As a pedestrian, you are also protected if you are hit by an uninsured vehicle.

No-Fault Insurance

Many states have passed no-fault insurance laws. These laws do not require a legal determination of who was at fault.

- *Purpose:* To provide medical and repair coverage from insurance company regardless of who is at fault.

Below is a chart that summarizes the above information. Our students find it much easier to refer to the chart as they begin to understand car insurance.

		Is Policyholder Protected?	Are Other People Protected?
Liability Coverage	Personal Injuries	No	Yes
	Property Damage	No	Yes
Collision Coverage	Damage to insured vehicle	Yes	No
Comprehensive Coverage	Damage to insured vehicle	Yes	No
Personal Injury Protection	Medical Payments	Yes	Yes
	Pedestrian Coverage	Yes	No
Uninsured/Underinsured Motorist Coverage			
	Bodily Injury	Yes	Yes

Step #3: Share with your teenager the details about auto insurance in your household

Now is the time to share with your teen about your own family's car insurance snapshot. Find the most recent policy for each of your cars and help your teenager find the premiums for each type of insurance you pay for. Have your teenager fill in the chart below. Be sure they understand the period of time that each premium covers (monthly, semi-annually, annually).

Explain to your teenager that these costs will vary depending on the factors noted earlier such as driving distance, number of drivers, make and model of the car. The best way to estimate your teenager's future insurance costs would be to contact your current agent or insurance company and ask for a quote. This will help your teenager better understand what their actual premium might be.

YOUR FAMILY'S CAR INSURANCE

	Car #1	Car #2	Car #3
Insurance Company:			
Period of Coverage:			
Liability Coverage			
Collision Coverage			
Comprehensive Coverage			
Personal Injury Protection			
Uninsured/Underinsured Motorist Coverage			

Step #4: Getting a new or used car? Make your teenager a part of the process.

If you are planning on buying or leasing a car for your teenager include him or her in the process. They'll come away with a much better understanding of how major a decision this is.   Also it's a great opportunity for your child to learn first-hand how big financial decisions take focus and research.   Go through the steps below before you head off to a dealership or used car lot. This will not only help de-mystify the process but also temper the thrill of having a new (or used) car. Just like opening a bank account, applying for a credit card or a student loan, the message here is that car ownership is an opportunity, but one that comes with responsibilities and often, serious financial obligations. It's not just 'magic'.

If you are not planning on buying or leasing a car in the near future, save this lesson until the time is right.

Step #5: Buy or lease? Which is better?

Before you start shopping, have a discussion with your teenager about how they will use the car and what is important to them about having a car.

* Is having a new car every 2-3 years more important than long term cost?

* Is having no major repair risks of value to you?

* How much will the car be driven, in terms of mileage?

* Is customizing the car important?

* Is pride of ownership a factor?

* Is having no car payment, in the future, something you find appealing?

* How willing are you to keep the car clean and the interior in good condition?

If always having the latest car is important to you, then leasing a car makes the most sense. Buying a new car every 2-3 years will be far more expensive for you than leasing one.

Leased cars are always under warranty and so the risk of repair is greatly reduced. Cars that are purchased will have limited warrantees and you will pay for most of the repairs over the time you own the car.

Generally speaking, if you drive more than 10,000 – 15,000 miles per year, a lease may not be your best option. Leases specify the number of miles you may drive per year and if you exceed that amount, you will be charged extra fees that could add up to significant dollars.

If you lease a car, you must return it in the same manner as you got it. If you've added rims or a new sound system, you will have to pay to restore the car to the original condition or the dealer will charge you fees.

Are you someone who just likes the idea of 'owning' their own car? Knowing it's yours (assuming you pay off the loan) and that some day you may even sell it and get some money for it? Then leasing is **not** for you. Remember, once a lease is up, you must give the car back. You then must enter into a new lease or decide on other means of transportation. The only money you may receive back from leasing would be your security deposit.

Is the idea of having no car payments in the future appealing to you? Then buying is the right choice. Assuming you take care of your car, once you've paid off the loan, you will have no more monthly payments. Of course, you will still pay for repairs, maintenance and insurance but those costs will be much lower than the combined total of monthly payments during the same period.

If you aren't particularly careful about keeping your car clean and keeping the interior in good condition, then leasing will cost you extra money at the end of the lease. The dealer will charge you to bring the car back up to good condition.

Step #6: Determine what you or your teenager can comfortably afford.

This is THE most important step when considering buying or leasing of a car. If the car is for your teenager, take a look at the budgets you helped your teen put together in Chapters 6.   Ask your teenager:

- Is there any extra money in the budget for a car payment? If not, are there any expenses that can be reduced? By how much – realistically?

- Is there any money in your teen's saving or checking account that may serve as a down payment?   If not, where will money for a down payment come from?

- Is there any extra money in that budget for car insurance, car repairs and maintenance? If not, where will that money come from?

At this point, you and your teen may have no idea about the amounts it will take to answer the above questions, but it's good to get your teenager to focus on how many potential expenses there are with the purchase or lease of a car.

Whether you are planning on taking out a loan, or leasing a new car, let your teen know what monthly amount you are comfortable with and how much of a down payment you can pay. If you are paying cash for a car, let them know. Have this discussion BEFORE you go car shopping!

Step #7: Credit Check

If you will be applying for a loan or a lease, show your teen how to check their/your credit score. Explain that a credit score is used to predict the likelihood that you will repay the loan or lease. It also determines the interest rate you will be offered on the loan or lease. Scores range from 300 to 850 and explain that people receive the best loan or lease package with scores above 700, generally speaking. It is important for the teen to know that the credit score is based on a credit report generated by three main credit bureaus: Equifax, Experian, and Transunion. Everyone may check their credit report from each of these companies three times a year for free by visiting www.annualcreditreport.com. Take the time to do this with your teenager and show them how to read a report. This will impress upon them the need to always pay on time, keep balances on credit cards low, and use credit regularly. These three things, along with time, will help your teen build a good credit score.

Step #8: Start Shopping

- Start with a little research on line. Decide which kinds of cars you are interested in and compare their features and costs. Read some reviews.

- Once you feel you've narrowed down the options, it's time to take your teen to the dealership or used car lot and test drive these cars.

- Write down the makes and models of the cars, the **MSRP (manufacturer's suggested retail price – sticker price)**, and the gas mileage.

- Find out if the dealership or car lot offers financing and leasing plans. Sit down with a sales person and have them explain what kinds of deals, loan and lease options, interest rates and down payments are associated with the cars you are most interested in.

- Ask about government incentives available for purchasing a certain type of car. Explain to your teen how this can save money.

- **Don't commit to anything during this first trip!** Go home, talk about what you learned – the pros and cons of each car. Talking through everything will help your teenager understand all the things there are to consider.   Getting away from the dealership will reduce the pressure and frenzy of making an emotional decision too hastily.

- Consider other loan options. Call your bank or credit union to determine if it might be able to offer you a better loan package than the dealership.   Share that information with

BUY USED!

Automotive technology instructor Manolo Lopez advises most people to buy used cars. He says, "Virtually all cars depreciate about 20% in value the first year. Therefore, if you're going to buy a car, don't buy a new car – ever. Rather, buy a 1 to 2 year old car in good condition. The major components will be under warranty for a while. It will still drive and smell like new. In essence, you're buying a new-ish car at a 20% discount."

your teenager.   They will understand that there is more than one place to get a loan and that shopping around can often save money in the long run.

Step #9: Consider the Other Costs

- Call your insurance agent and find out the cost of adding another car to your policy. Share this information with your teenager.

- Remind your teenager that other costs such as repairs, maintenance, taxes and fees could add up to hundreds of dollars annually.

CAR LOAN COMPARISON

	Car #1 Example	Car #2	Car #3	Car #4
MSRP or Best Price Possible	$20,000			
Sales Tax - 7.0%	$1,400			
Down Payment Amount	$5,000			
Amount of Loan (MSRP - Down Payment)	$16.400			
Loan Term (Number of Months)	60 months			
Interest Rate	6%			
Monthly Payment (Write down the payment generated by the loan calculator)	$317.06			
Total Interest Paid (After 60 months)	$2,623.48			
Approx. Total Cost of Car ((Down Payment + (Monthly payment x no. of months)	$24,023.60			

Step #10: Run the Numbers for a Car Loan

Now that you have a good idea about how much money you will need to borrow to buy a new car, teach your teen how to use a loan calculator and how a loan works. Go to www.bankrate.com and click on calculators or auto and find an auto loan calculator with **amortization schedule** (an amortization schedule will show you every payment you will make on a loan and how much of the payment will go toward paying off the principal – the loan amount – and how much will go toward paying off the interest – the price of the loan.)

For example, if you assume the purchase price of the car is $20,000, sales tax is 7% ($1,400), the down payment is $5,000, and the loan amount is $16,400. The loan term is 5 years (60 months), the interest rate is 6% per year, the monthly payment will be $317.06.

By scrolling down through the amortization table, your teenager will see every payment laid out for 5 years. Our students are always amazed by the fact that you will pay more in interest up front and by how much interest adds up over the length of the loan. Be sure to point out the final number in the Total Interest column of the amortization table. In this case the Total Interest is $2,623.48.

Have your teenager fill in the *Car Loan Comparison* chart to emphasize the costs involved in the purchase of a car.

Step #11: How to Reduce the Cost of a Loan

Now that your teenager is beginning to understand how a loan works and what the costs are, explain that there are ways to reduce the cost of a loan. They are:

- Buy a cheaper car! (How's that for a concept?!)

- Increase the down payment – you will pay less in interest

- Find a lower interest rate – shop around

- Choose a shorter term loan – the monthly payment will be higher, but you will pay less in interest overall

Now ask your teen, **Can we reduce the cost of a loan on this car?** Talk about it.

Step #12: Understanding a Car Lease

Even if your family leases its cars, most teenagers have no idea what leasing is all about. Explain that when you lease a car, you are not paying for the entire car. You will be paying for the amount of the car you 'use up' while driving it – also known

as the **depreciated amount**.

You will also need to explain a few terms that your teenager has probably never heard of.

Capitalized cost: Sometimes called the **lease price**. This is the price for the leased car. In a good lease deal, the capitalized cost is significantly less than MSRP.

Residual Value: At the end of a lease a car will have a wholesale value known as the residual value. The higher the residual value, the lower your lease payments will be. Why? *Because the leasing company can get more money for the car at the end of the lease.* Residual values are often stated as a percentage of MSRP. For example, a 50% residual on a new $20,000 car means that the estimated residual value at the end of the lease will be $10,000.

Money Factor: Also known as the **lease rate**. The leasing company will expect you to pay interest on the money they had to pay for the car in the first place. The money factor is expressed as a small decimal such as .00297. But don't be fooled! This does not mean that the interest rate is really low (the dealer may try to confuse you by telling you the money factor is 2.97 to make you think it's 2.97% and therefore a great rate.) In order to compare money factors to interest rates you must first multiply the money factor by 2400. In this example, .00297 x 2400 = 7.13%. Now you may compare the 7.13% with interest rates offered on car loans. You should expect to get the same rate or lower than a new-car loan interest rate.

Remember, the lower the money factor, the lower the lease payment!

AGAIN, BUY USED!

The automotive technology instructor at our high school, Manolo Lopez, advises the following: "If you're going to buy your kid a car, buy them a very used car. Almost every kid I know under the age of 25 gets into at least one accident – most of them occur in the first year of driving! And it's no secret as to why this happens – they are inexperienced and don't know how to avoid many dangerous situations. The parents and the kid won't feel quite as bad about damaging a very used car rather than a new car."

Security Deposit: Most dealers will require a lump sum of money as collateral for the lease.

These are the main concepts of leasing. There are more terms and aspects to a lease deal but the point is not to overwhelm your teenager. You've covered all the important basics.

Step #13: Run the Numbers for a Car Lease

Go to www.bankrate.com and click on calculators. Then choose Buy or Lease a Car. This is a great tool that allows you to compare a loan to a lease. In our leasing example, the purchase price is $20,000, the down payment is $5,000 and the sales tax is 7% (this will vary depending on where you live.) In the box labeled Investment Rate of Return, we assume 8%. This is the return you would make if you invested rather than use your money on a down payment or security deposit. It's important that your teenager always think about what their money could be making if they weren't spending it!

In our example we assume a lease term of 36 months, an interest rate of 6% (derived from a money factor of .0025 x 2400), fees of $100, a residual value of 50%, and a security deposit of $500. Using this information, the monthly lease payment will be $290.62 per month. Now calculate the total cost of the lease. (See chart on next page for calculation.)

Have your teenager fill in the *Car Lease Comparison* chart to emphasize the costs involved in leasing a car.

Step #14: How to Reduce the Cost of a Lease

Now that your teenager is beginning to understand how a lease works and what the costs are, explain that there are ways to reduce the cost of a lease. They are:

*   Lease a cheaper car!
*   Make a larger down payment
*   Lease a car with a higher residual value
*   Shop around for a lower money factor

Now ask your teen if you can reduce the cost of the lease on any of the cars above. Talk about it.

CAR LEASE COMPARISON

	Car #1 Example	Car #2	Car #3	Car #4
Capitalized Cost	$20,000			
Sales Tax	$1,400 (7%)			
Down Payment	$5,000			
Money Factor x 2400 (Approx. Interest Rate)	.0025 x 2400 = 6% (Example assumes a money factor of .0025)			
Residual Value	50%			
Term of Lease	36 months			
Security Deposit	$500			
Dealer Fees	$100			
Monthly Lease Payment	$290.62			
Total Cost of the Lease ((Down Payment + (# of months x lease payment))	$5,000 + (36 x $290.62) =$15,462.32			

Step #15: Negotiate in Confidence

Now that you and your teen have a good idea about the costs and benefits of each car you are considering, return to the dealership. Do your best to strike a good deal. Explain to your teen that dealers will usually agree to discount the sticker price and that it is okay to haggle. This may not hold true if the vehicle is in high demand and supply is low. Point out to your teen that a buyer is in much better control of the deal if they have done their homework. While it takes time, it will save you lots of money in the long run and you will feel better about the decision you made.

Chapter Eight Checklist:

Check off the items you and your teenager have completed:

☐ 1.   Fill in the chart of gas consumption of your family's car(s).

☐ 2.   Fill in the chart of other costs of your family's car(s).

☐ 3.   Review the types of car insurance.

☐ 4.   Review your family's car insurance costs.

☐ 5.   Compare the costs of loans for 3 cars.

☐ 6.   Compare the costs of leases for 3 cars.

☐ 7.   Discuss ways to lower costs of owning or leasing a car.

Notes

Chapter 9
THIS IS GOING TO HURT:
Taxes and Why They Matter

"I love to go to Washington, if only to be nearer my money."

- Bob Hope

THIS IS GOING TO HURT:
Taxes and Why They Matter

GOAL: To have teens learn how to estimate their future yearly tax liability and how to determine their required paycheck deductions.

Let's face it: taxes are about the most boring and unsexy money topic there is. But as adults, we all know that taxes never go away and, in fact, are an important piece of life's major financial decisions. In order for your teen to fully understand how much money they take home vs. earn and their legal and financial responsibilities, it is vital that they begin to appreciate what happens to their paycheck and how to plan for their yearly tax liability. As teachers, we know that once our students learn how to calculate taxes and read their own paycheck stubs, they become fully engaged in the whole topic. In fact, their reactions are almost always the same: "Taxes are too high and too complex!"

Step #1: Gross Pay is a Fantasy

Have your teenager guess how much money they would have leftover **after** paying taxes if they earned $30,000 in one year. The answer is

approximately $24,000. Most teenagers will be shocked. They want to know where the $6,000 went and here's your chance to tell them.

Start by having your teen imagine their future profession and a reasonable salary they may be earning after college. These figures have a bigger WOW factor than earnings from a minimum wage job and it will more significantly illustrate the effect taxes have on an individual's take-home pay.

Have your teenager look back at Chapter 4, *WHERE'S YOUR PASSION? Research Careers, What They Pay, and the Skills and the Education You Need*

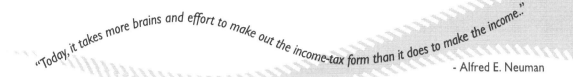

"Today, it takes more brains and effort to make out the income-tax form than it does to make the income."

- Alfred E. Neuman

to *Be Successful.* In the chart on page 164, have them record the annual earnings from their research on several careers. (If they picked a career that is paid hourly, multiply the hourly rate by 2,000 hours to get annual earnings.)

Explain to your teen that in the world of personal finance, annual earnings are also known as **gross pay.** That is the amount of your pay **before** any deductions.

Also explain there are **4 required deductions** for most people who work: Federal Income Tax, State Income Tax (there are a few states that don't have an income tax), Social Security tax, and Medicare tax. (There may be other required deductions depending on your state and there may be other deductions chosen by the employee. We do not, however, want to overwhelm your teenager at this point with too many details.)

Federal income taxes provide the federal government with revenue to pay for things like national defense, our interstate highway system, national parks, and medical research. The U.S. has a **progressive tax** system which means that individuals with higher taxable income are taxed at a higher rate than individuals with lower

DOLLARS & $ENSE

According to Andy Levinson, CPA and Partner at the accounting firm Gish Seiden LLP, the biggest mistake parents make when it comes to teaching their kids about taxes is "not teaching them anything at all. My clients shield their kids from the whole process for years. Most parents never show or have their kids sign their own tax returns. College kids and graduates who aren't dealing with their own taxes are just delaying reality."

Andy Levinson goes on to say that "these kids grow up to become adults who lack any real understanding of how the tax system works in our country. Most adults have the misconception that what is taken out (taxes) is what they owe when in fact, it's often the case they owe a quite a bit more. Therefore, it's important to know what you are going to owe at the beginning of the year, not at the end."

taxable incomes. Generally how much tax you pay depends on how much you earn, minus certain deductions. Of course it is more complicated than that, but most college graduates will have a fairly simple financial picture. Your employer is required by law to deduct a portion of these taxes from your paycheck throughout the year.

Step #2: Meet the IRS!

Get your computer and go to: www.irs.gov. Explain to your teenager that **IRS** stands for **Internal Revenue Service** and that this is the federal government agency that collects taxes. Also explain that everyone who works in the U.S. is required to file a **tax return** by April 15 of the year after you earned income. A tax return is a form that reflects all the income earned, taxes paid, and other financially related information that the IRS requires. Tax return does NOT mean that you will have taxes returned to you! The name of the tax return your student will most likely use by the time they are working in their 'dream' career, is Form 1040. (This is because we assume they will be contributing to an IRA, they may have student loans on which they are paying interest, and they may be contributing to a charitable organization.) In the search box, type: 1040 and print out a copy of the form for your teenager to look over.

Explain to your teen that all tax returns are intimidating, complicated, and confusing. But it's important to understand the basics even if you hire an accountant or service to complete the forms for you. Otherwise, how do you know if you're getting ripped off?

In the search box, type: 1040 instructions. Ex-

plain to your teenager that the 1040 instructions contain step-by-step information about how to fill out the form as well as the tax tables that will show you how much tax you would be required to pay if:

- Your **taxable income** is less than $100,000. Taxable income is different from gross pay. **Taxable income** is the income on which you are required to pay tax. It's your gross pay minus certain deductions. In this lesson the only tax deduction we are assuming is the standard deduction: $5,700, in 2011. Of course, there can be more tax deductions that may apply, but we're trying to keep this simple and reasonable.

- You contribute to an IRA – which we strongly recommend starting at age 18. (Chapter 10 will explain that in more detail.)

- You are paying off a student loan with interest.

- You make charitable donations.

There are other reasons and restrictions for using the 1040, but we're assuming that most young adults will be using this form at least at the beginning of their careers. During high school and college, most students who work part-time will use the 1040EZ. We will talk about the 1040EZ a little later in this chapter.

In the table of contents for the 1040 Instructions, find Tax Tables and go to that page. Then scroll down until you find the taxable income you calculated in the chart on page 148 for each career; gross pay minus $5,700 – the standard deduction in 2011 - or whatever standard deduction applies.

Step #3: Your State Wants A Cut of the Action Too!

State income taxes provide state governments with revenue to pay for things like universities, roads, hospitals, schools and court systems. States also typically have a progressive income tax (like the Federal system) and base your tax obligations (i.e. how much you owe) on your income minus deductions. Your employer is required by law to deduct a portion of these taxes from your paycheck throughout the year.

Go to your state's website and search for instructions that will tell you what your state's standard deduction is for a single person with no dependents. Subtract your state's standard deduction from your hypothetical $30,000 gross pay to get your taxable income. Record that in the chart. Then search your state's website for the tax tables and find the amount associated with your taxable income. Record it in the chart.

Step #4: And There's Still More...

Social Security taxes provide federal aid (money) for the elderly and for disabled individuals. How much you pay is calculated like this: Your gross pay x 6.2%. So, if you made $30,000 in one year, you would punch into your calculator 30,000 x .062 = $1,860. Now calculate your own social security tax and record that number in the chart. Your employer is required to deduct a portion of these taxes from your paycheck throughout the year.

Medicare taxes provide hospital and medical insurance for elderly retired individuals and for some disabled individuals. How much you pay is

> ## Tax Freedom Day:
> The first day of the year in which a nation as a whole has theoretically earned enough income to fund its annual tax burden. In 2011, the day was April 12. In other words, Americans worked well over 3 months of the year before they have earned enough to pay 2011's tax obligations.

calculated like this: Your gross pay x 1.45%. So, if you made $30,000 in one year, you would punch into your calculator 30,000 x .0145 = $435. Now calculate your own Medicare tax and record that number in the chart. Your employer is required to deduct a portion of these taxes from your paycheck throughout the year.

Finally, take your gross pay and subtract:

- Federal income tax
- State tax (if applicable)
- Social security tax
- Medicare tax

The number you are left with is your **net pay** also known as **take-home pay**. In the example, your gross pay is $30,000 but your net pay – what you really have available to spend, pay bills with, save and invest – is about $24,000. That's right, you don't get to keep all of it. And remember, the higher your taxable income, the more taxes you will pay. **Net pay** is the dollar amount you should use to plan your budget – how much you have to live on for the year.

POTENTIAL TAX OBLIGATION COMPARISON

	Example	Career #1	Career #2	Career #3
Annual Earnings aka **Gross Pay**	$30,000			
Taxable Income Estimate (use gross pay and subtract $5,700. $5,700 is the standard deduction for a single person in 2011)	$24,300 ($30,000 - $5,700 = $24,300)			
Federal Income Taxes	$3,231			
State Income Taxes (Our example assumes California state tax)	$717 ($30,000 – standard deduction = taxable income)			
Social Security Taxes (gross pay x 6.2%)	$1,507 ($24,300 x .062)			
Medicare Taxes (gross pay x 1.45%)	$352 ($24,300 x .0145)			
Net Pay aka Take - Home Pay (estimate)	**$24,193** ($30,000 - $3,231 - $717 - $1,507 - $352 = $24,193)			

Note: The tax amounts used in the above example are based on 2011 tax information.

"INTAXICATION: Euphoria at getting a refund from the IRS, which lasts until you realize it was your money to start with.."

- Author Unknown

(From a *Washington Post* word contest)

Tying It All Together

In Chapter 6 you and your teen put together a realistic budget depending on their post-high school plans. Explain that in the future, your teen should develop a household budget similar to the one they made for college but making sure to deduct their potential tax obligation before they figure out how much money they have for expenses.

Because we are all taxed on our **taxable income**, the object of the tax-game is to find legal ways to lower your taxable income. There are many ways to do this – mostly through investing, creating your own business, buying a home or condo, and making charitable donations. In Chapter 10, *A LITTLE NOW, A LATTE LATER: Saving and Investing For Your Future,* your teenager will learn how to begin the saving/investing process that will help your teenager to shelter income from some federal and state taxes.

But the important thing your teen should learn is to plan their life and their budget around their net pay NOT their gross pay. Taking a few minutes every year to estimate your annual tax liability is critical to making smart decisions with your money.

Before you move on, be sure that your teenager understands that the net pay calculated in the chart is based on annual earnings from a future career.

Step #5: What About the Present?

If your teenager currently has a job it is important for you to get one of his/her paycheck stubs and together identify the following: (Warning: employers may use different names for some of these. If you are unsure which deduction is which, have your teen call the person in charge of payroll and ask – a great learning experience, by the way.)

- Pay period (weekly, bi-weekly, semi-monthly, monthly)

- Gross pay

- The 4 required deductions (Federal income tax, state income tax, Medicare and Social Security taxes)

- Any other deductions (such as disability insurance, pension plans)

- Net Pay

Refer to Publication 15 at the IRS website. Publication 15 breaks down federal income tax liability by pay period. This can help your teen to better plan out their budget. Have your teenager use the tax tables for the pay period that applies to their job and help them find their federal income tax withholding on the chart. Then compare that number to the federal income tax number on their pay stub and see if they match. Do the same for state income tax withholding. If the amounts don't match, your teen might need to change their

DOLLARS & $ENSE

Mary Hogan, a self-employed accountant, warns that many people receive bonuses throughout their careers and assume that the correct amount of taxes are withheld at the time the bonus is paid. They later come to find out that only a fraction of the legal amount owed was withheld and therefore, end up with a huge tax bill at the end of the year. "I once prepared the tax return of a Hollywood executive who received a $100,000 bonus. He assumed that the company withheld the proper amount of taxes and spent the rest of the money. When it came time to prepare his taxes, I determined that he owed approximately $20,000 in taxes on the bonus alone. He had to take out a loan to pay the IRS."

allowances on **Form W4** and give a new one to their employer. **Form W4** is a form completed by an employee to determine the amount the employer will withhold from your paycheck for income taxes. The employer sends this money to the government. By having the correct number of allowances stated on a Form W4, your teenager won't end up owing taxes at the end of the year or having too much taken out throughout the year. Remember that it's important to stress that they are legally liable for the amount stated on the chart. Note: Many teenagers working part-time are exempt from paying Federal income taxes and will get a refund after they file. This is actually a good 'forced savings plan' for them.

If your teenager/student doesn't have an IRA or a student loan yet, then most likely they will be filling out Form 1040EZ at tax time. Explain that failure to complete a tax return is called **tax eva-**

sion and may result in fines, jail time or both. Go to the IRS website, print out a copy of the Form 1040EZ . Compare the 1040 with the 1040EZ. While it is shorter in length, it is still confusing for our students and for most adults. Explain to your teen that after January 1 of the year following the current year, they will receive a **Form W2** in the mail from their employer. Form W2 will summarize all taxes and withholding for the year. Your teen will need the Form W2 to complete their tax return. Here is another opportunity for you and your teenager to learn about another area of personal finance together. Help them do their own taxes. It's not so complex that you can't both be successful.

If you prefer to have your accountant or tax service prepare your teenager's tax return, have your teenager meet with them and have the professional explain the return to your teen. Have your

"Did you ever notice that when you put the words 'The' and 'IRS' together, it spells 'THEIRS'?"

- Author unknown

teen sign their own forms and pay for the service. This will help them understand the full process in both time and money.

You may also choose to share with your teen a past tax return of your own. You can show them what Form W2 and a completed tax return look like.

One final note: We have tried to make this lesson on taxes as simple and straightforward as possible. Taxes are difficult to understand and complicated to compute and we have found that it takes many years for most people to understand how the whole process actually works. But you should feel great that you have started your teenager on that process early!

We have long had death and taxes as the two standards of inevitability. But there are those who believe that death is the preferable of the two. "At least," as one man said, "there's one advantage about death; it doesn't get worse every time Congress meets."

- Erwin N. Griswold

Chapter Nine Checklist:

Check off the items you and your teenager have completed:

☐ 1. Understand the difference between gross pay and net pay.

☐ 2. Know how to look up federal and state annual income tax liability online.

☐ 3. Know the purpose of filing a tax return.

☐ 4. Understand how to read a paycheck stub.

☐ 5. Know how to look up federal state income tax withholding online.

Notes

Chapter 10

A LITTLE NOW, A LATTE LATER:

Saving and Investing for Your Future

"If you are not willing to own stock for 10 years, don't even think about owning it for 10 minutes."

- Warren Buffet

A LITTLE NOW, A LATTE LATER:
Saving & Investing for Your Future

GOAL: To have teens begin saving (in addition to a regular savings account) and investing.

Saving money means putting money away for the future. Whether you're saving for a car, college, or to buy stock, you must first decide NOT to spend that money today. Saving is hard. It is not fun. It is not glamorous. It is a lot easier not to save. Saving takes discipline and sacrifice – both of which teenagers are NOT very good at. They've had little practice and often, few role models.

We feel that this lesson - on saving and investing - is the most critical lesson you can teach your teenager. Why? **Because saving and investing is the only sure way to build wealth and to give yourself options in life.** If you buy a car, you have more freedom about where you can work and when you can go places. If you go to college, you have more career choices and the ability to earn more money. If you buy stock, bonds or mutual funds you may earn money while you own them. Then you can use that money to buy more stock, bonds or mutual funds or invest in other things that may earn even more money. The paycheck from your job becomes less critical and your sense of financial freedom will grow.

It's now time to take your teenager through the basics of saving and investing. This topic can get complex quickly, so we've tried to keep it very simple and straightforward.

DOLLARS & $ENSE

Meet Bill. While Bill was in high school he opened his first regular savings account. During his summers, Bill worked as a lifeguard on Long Island Sound. He deposited his weekly paychecks in his account and saved for college.

At 18 Bill's father insisted that Bill open an IRA (individual retirement account – a type of savings-investing plan) at Fidelity Brokerage Services. Putting aside the maximum allowed by law, Bill faithfully deposited $2,000 that year and the money was invested in mutual funds which are investments into a variety of stocks and bonds.

The year was 1975. The Vietnam War ended, Motorola filed the first patent for a mobile phone, Bruce Springsteen released the album "Born To Run," the movie "Jaws" came out, "Starsky and Hutch" began its television run and Gerald Ford was President.

During college, Bill continued to life guard during the summers and he continued to make the $2,000 deposit into his Fidelity account. After college, Bill worked for a few years then headed back to graduate school, taking out student loans to pay his way. Though he was still paying off his undergraduate loans he continued to work at odd jobs and make the annual deposit to his IRA. This wasn't easy but Bill had discipline and lived simply.

After graduate school, Bill began his career in commercial real estate. It was a good paying career from the start. However, while most of his colleagues traded up to luxury cars, Bill continued to drive his old Subaru and later upgraded to a Toyota Camry. While most of his colleagues were renting large apartments and buying furniture and electronics, Bill stayed in his sparsely furnished studio apartment. While most of his colleagues had a closet full of nice business suits, Bill had two. "I bought a lot of ties to make them look different", he told our students recently, half laughing.

Not that Bill lived like a monk; he skied regularly, he went out for nice dinners occasionally and traveled a bit. But he enjoyed all of these things on a modest level and he continued to make the $2,000 deposit every year to his IRA.

Throughout the 70s, and 80s, the mutual funds that Bill owned through his IRA gained in value, lost in value, earned dividends and interest and didn't earn dividends and interest. Bill sold some of the funds, but immediately bought others. More often than not, the funds made money. He never withdrew any money from the account.

In 1992 Bill stopped contributing money to the Fidelity IRA. He opened another IRA with another brokerage firm and deposited money there instead. He also had other investments that he was contributing money to on a regular basis. But the Fidelity account continued to exist and the funds continued to make and lose money. More often than not, the account made money for Bill. Here is his Fidelity account "report card" in 2010.

- *Bill's Fidelity account is worth approximately $100,000.*

- *He made deposits for 17 years*

- *He deposited a total of $34,000*

- *He earned $66,000 from the investment –*
  DID 'YA CATCH THAT? He made $66,000 of "free" money by investing $34,000. That's nearly trippling his money!

- *Bill never withdrew any money from the account*

How is Bill doing at age 50? Bill is a successful commercial real estate executive. He drives a high-end BMW, lives in a nice home with his family, travels, still enjoys skiing, eats at really nice restaurants on a regular basis, and owns more than two suits. In fact, many of them are hand made suits. In addition to the Fidelity account, he has another IRA, a 401K plan (another savings-investment account), owns a small apartment building and is a partner in several other office buildings. His two children are in high school. Bill and his wife are able to pay for their college educations.

This is a story about how money can grow over time – also known as the compounding effect of money. It seems like magic, but it's more about discipline and sacrifice. Bill isn't a financial genius – you don't have to be. But, you must begin the process NOW.

*There is an old saying; **"Time is money."** Remember those three simple words and think of them every time you make a deposit.*

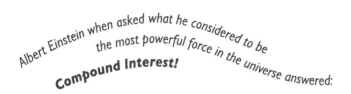

Albert Einstein when asked what he considered to be the most powerful force in the universe answered: **Compound Interest!**

Step #1: The Basics

For most people, the first place they save is in a 'regular' **savings account** at a bank or credit union. Money deposited in a savings account is called **principal**. A bank then lends out most of that money to other people and businesses. (Assure your teen that the money in most banks is insured by the Federal government and the banks are able to get money quickly in case they need it.)

A **'Regular' Savings Account**: When you deposit money into a savings account, the bank pays you something called **interest**. Interest is always expressed as an annual percent, for example, 1.5%. Suppose you deposit $100 into your regular savings account and let it sit there for one year. The bank will pay you 1.5% in interest ($100 x .015 = $1.50). The interest earned is $1.50. Next, they add the interest to your beginning balance ($1.50 + $100 = $101.50). The ending balance is $101.50. In year 2, the bank applies the 1.5% interest rate but this time it's applied to BOTH principal and interest ($101.50 x .015). By calculating interest on both the principal and the interest added together, the banks are paying you compound interest.

Show your teenager how the bank calculates the interest if it is compounded annually over three years:

$100 Deposit Earning 1.5% for 3 Years

Year	Beginning Balance	Interest Earned (1.5%)	Ending Balance
1	$100 (deposit)	$1.50	$101.50
2	$101.50	$1.52	$103.02
3	$103.02	$1.54	$104.56

You earned a whopping $4.56 in three years for depositing $100. Not too exciting, is it? Our students always tell us how ridiculous this seems. And they always ask, **"How can we make more money with our money?"**

Step #2: The Magic of Compound Interest
Go through the following tables with your Teen

There are three ingredients needed to make money on your money: **time, interest rate, and principal**. Let's look at other interest rates and add more time. Suppose you deposit $100 that earns 1.5%, 3% and 11%. And further suppose you don't use any of that money for 50 years (no withdrawals).

Here's how much money you'll have after every ten years:

$100 Deposit Earning Different Interest Rates for 50 Years

Year	Ending Balance earning 1.5%	Ending Balance earning 3%	Ending Balance earning 11%
10	$116	$134	$283
20	$134	$180	$806
30	$156	$242	$2,289
40	$181	$326	$6,500
50	$210	$438	$18,456

Our students immediately focus on the $18,456 ending balance. And someone always yells out, "I'd have $18,456 by just depositing $100 today? Where can I earn 11%?" The answer is the stock market. But let's not get ahead of ourselves — more on that in a minute.

Even with 1.5% interest compounded annually, you would double your money in 50 years. Think about that — doubling your money for doing nothing but leaving it in the bank. What would happen to that same $100 if you put it in a desk drawer for 50 years? Nothing (actually, due to the effects of inflation, that money will lose value and be worth less). There's the magic! But think bigger. What if you saved more than $100? What if you saved $100 every year?

Let's look at the numbers one more time:

$100 Deposited Every Year at Different Interest Rates for 50 Years

Year	Ending Balance earning 1.5%	Ending Balance earning 3%	Ending Balance earning 11%
10	$743	$1,180	$1,856
20	$2,347	$2,767	$7,126
30	$3,810	$4,900	$22,091
40	$5,508	$7,766	$64,582
50	$7,478	$11,618	$185,233

Our students love these numbers! Someone usually shouts out, "I could save more than $100 every year. I'll be earning some serious cashmoney by the time I'm in my late 20s!"

The Rule of 72

A simple concept called "The Rule of 72" illustrates the dramatic way money can grow if you just give it enough time. The Rule will show you how long it will take for your money to double.

Example: How long will it take for $1,000 to double if it earns 2% interest? You find the answer like this: 72 ÷ 2 = 36 years

In 36 years you will have $2,000.

How about 11% interest? 72 ÷ 11 = 6.5 years

In 6.5 years you will have $2,000.

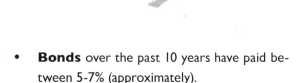

But back to the question of interest rates and where you can get higher ones:

- **Regular savings accounts** over the past 10 years have paid between .05 and 2% (approximately).

- **Certificates of deposit accounts** over the past 10 years have paid between 1% and 5% (approximately).

- **Money-market accounts** over the past 10 years have paid between 1% and 5% (approximately).

- **Bonds** over the past 10 years have paid between 5-7% (approximately).

Then there are stocks that don't pay interest but your money has the potential to make more money for you over time. This is known as the **compounding effect of money** and it is measured by its **rate of return**, expressed as a percent.

- The **stock market** has delivered an average of 10% annual growth (the increased value of stocks) for most of the last century.

Step #3: The Mainstream Investment World At a Glance!

This next section can become overwhelming for most teenagers if given all at one time. We suggest that you cover this section after taking a break. And we also suggest that you share some information with your teen about any investments you may have. If you own stock, tell them how much you bought it for, when you bought it and how it has performed. Do the same with any other investments you may have and share that history, losses as well as gains.

Let's talk about some basic investment types:

A **regular savings account** may be started at a bank or credit union. The Federal government insures almost all banks and credit unions and this protects your deposits up to $250,000. All banks and credit unions pay interest that often compounds daily.

A **certificate of deposit – CD** – is a deposit that earns a fixed interest rate (one that doesn't change) for a specified length of time. For example, 3% for six months. A CD requires a minimum deposit. The interest rate is higher than on regular savings accounts because CDs are less **liquid**. That means you must leave your money in the account for the full period to earn the full amount of interest. The banks are willing to pay you more interest because they know you won't be taking it out and therefore, they can lend out that money more easily.

A **money market account** is a combination savings-investment plan in which money deposited is used to purchase safe, IOUs from the U.S. government. For the use of your money, the government pays interest. The chance of losing your money is very low in a money market account. Some money market accounts are insured, some are not. The uninsured accounts usually pay higher interest rates. Money market accounts usually have a minimum deposit such as $500. Banks and **brokerage firms** offer money market accounts. At a brokerage firm you can invest in other things like stock, bonds, mutual funds and more. A brokerage firm may also advise you on investment decisions.

A **bond** is a loan to a company or to the government by you, the investor. The money you lend them is called **principal**. For the use of your money, the company or government will pay you a fixed rate (stays the same) of interest for the **term** (length of time) of the loan. At **maturity** (the end of the term) the principal is repaid. There are many types of bonds. Some pay high interest rates of interest, some pay low rates. You can spend anywhere from $50 to over $100,000+ on a bond. The term can range from a few weeks to thirty years. (For more information about bonds see the list of websites at the end of this chapter.)

Stock is ownership in a corporation. When you buy stock – or shares - you have an ownership share in that corporation and you are known as a **shareholder** or **stockholder**. When most people buy stock, they hope to sell it one day for a higher price than they paid. When that happens, it is known as a **capital gain**; our students often refer to it as 'profit'. When a stock is sold for less than the price paid, it is known as a **capital loss**. The price of stock moves up and down depending on how much other investors are willing to pay. You can also make money on stocks by receiving **dividends** – payments from the corporation out of its profit. Because you are an owner of the corporation, you get to share in the profits of the corporation. There are thousands of stocks available to buy. Some are considered more risky than others. The price of stocks may range from a penny to several hundred dollars or more. Some stocks pay consistent dividends, some never pay dividends. (For more information about stock see the list of websites at the end of this chapter.)

A **mutual fund** is a company that pools money from many investors and uses that money (a fund) to purchase a variety of stocks, bonds, and real estate. The fund makes money in two ways – by earning dividends or interest on its investments and by selling investments that have increased in price. You can invest in that fund by buying shares. You can make money from mutual funds in two ways:

1. From the income the fund earns on its investments and then pays out to investors (minus fees and expenses).

2. From the profits the fund earns by selling its investments and then pays out to investors (minus fees and expenses).

Since a fund is working with millions of dollars, they can buy hundreds of different investments consisting of a variety of stocks, bonds and real estate – it isn't dependent on just a few. Spreading out investments among many types and varieties is known as **diversification**. Many investment professionals agree that diversification is a smart way to limit your risk and still realize the compounding effect of money. There are thousands of mutual funds available to buy. Some are considered more risky than others. The price of mutual fund shares range from a few dollars to one hundred approximately. (For more information about mutual funds see the list of websites at the end of this chapter.)

Step #4: Playing With Live Ammo

Before he or she turns 18, have your teen try one of the following investments opportunities:

- Purchase a savings bond through your teen's bank.

- Do a little research and purchase $500 worth of stock.

- Open a CD account.

- Play a free virtual stock market game (we recommend virtualstockexchange.com) and learn about the stock market by picking your own stocks and watching their movement over time.

DOLLARS & $ENSE

KC, a 17 year old student in our finance class, loved clothes. Not just any clothes; crazy, unique combinations of garments. He often wore hunting caps, slippers, a rope belt (literally, a piece of white rope tied in a knot), snakeskin cowboy boots, velvet, etc.. Anything with faux fur? – Of course, that was a favorite of his.

How did he satisfy his clothing obsession? KC scoured garage sales, estate sales and flea markets. While normal teenagers were fast asleep on Saturday and Sunday mornings, KC would be up and off to the sales by 7:00 am. He knew the basics of supply and demand; the good stuff would be gone by 8:00 am.

But here's the best part. KC would over-buy all kinds of items, keep a few for himself and then re-sell the rest on ebay and Craig's list at prices higher than he paid. He even sold items he picked up for free.

*His dating life suffered - most girls don't gravitate toward frugal types - but he managed to outfit himself **and** have spending money throughout high school. Additionally, along with other earnings from odd jobs, KC invested in his first certificate of deposit, earning 4% during his senior year of high school.*

Step #5:
Retirement Saving is NOT for Old People

AFTER a teenager turns 18, help them open an Individual Retirement Account (IRA) and have them begin making contributions to it.

IRA BASICS
An **IRA** is a personal savings plan that gives you a tax break for participating. You must be 18 and earning income (part-time jobs and summer employment are fine) to open an IRA. You can open an IRA at a bank, a mutual fund company, or a brokerage firm.

If your teenager doesn't have some kind of a job at this point, we strongly recommend you insist they find one. Your teen cannot really begin to understand the value of money until they've worked for a paycheck. You can't teach that to them, it must be experienced first hand.

There are three types of IRAs:

1. Traditional deductible IRA: This is tax deferred which means you owe no tax on your earnings until you withdraw money (starting at age 59.5 at the earliest). You may deduct some or all of the money you contribute from your reported taxable income, depending on your marital status and income level.

2. Traditional non-deductible IRA: This is tax deferred which means you owe no tax on your earnings until you withdraw money (starting at age 59.5 at the earliest). You may not deduct your contributions from your reported income on a tax return.

3. Roth IRA: This is tax free which means you owe no tax on any earnings as they accumulate however, you will pay tax on contributions. Not everyone is eligible for a Roth, however. There are income and marital status rules that apply. The Roth was originally created for middle-income individuals. Check the IRS website at irs.gov for the most current information.

If you are under fifty, you may contribute the smaller of $5,000 or taxable compensation (income) each year. So, if your teenager makes $3,000 during the year through part-time jobs and/or summer work, they may contribute a maximum of $3,000. If they made $6,000, they may contribute a maximum of $5,000. (After 2010, the contribution limit will increase by $500 depending on the level of inflation.) You can make contributions whenever you like. Many people find it easiest to have **automatic payroll de-**

ductions every pay period. But for teens who are working sporadically, it's often best for them to make a yearly contribution from their regular savings or checking account. (That means that they cannot spend all the money they make!)

An IRA is **self-directed** which means you decide how to invest your money and you're responsible for knowing and following the rules that apply to the account. That really boils down to making the legal contribution and then reporting it on your tax forms correctly.

Step #6: Get a Little Help

You can invest your IRA money in a variety of investment types; from savings accounts to risky stock transactions. For beginners, we recommend mutual funds and therefore, we also recommend that you and your teenager sit down with a financial advisor at a brokerage firm and discuss some options and set up a realistic plan. If you already use a financial advisor consider having your teen meet with that person. If you don't have one, ask friends and family members for a recommendation and make an appointment! Go with your teenager to meet the advisor and learn together.

Many of our 18 year old students have part-time jobs and go on to work throughout college. We encourage all of them to open IRAs and to at least save a minimum of $500 every year – until they get their first REAL job, then they should save at least 10% of their earnings every paycheck using **automatic payroll deduction**.

Step #7: The Bottom Line
Be sure to share this with your teenager.

Start saving young, deposit often, find good interest rates, and diversify your investments. BUT, it is hugely important for you to know that the biggest factor in having your money grow to earn more money is TIME! Starting to save at an early age is absolutely critical. If you wait until you are 30 or 40 years old to start saving and investing, you will never come to close to earning the numbers shown in the charts above. Even small amounts in the early years make a giant difference. That's the magic of the compounding effect of money. If you don't believe us, take a look at this last chart.

	Jonathan	Michelle
Begins saving at age	18	39
Saves each year	$100	$200
Saves a total of	$5,000	$5,800
Interest rate	3%	3%
Total years of saving and investing	50 years	29 years
Total amount saved plus interest earned at age 68:	$11,618	$9,557

Do you see what happened? Jonathon started 11 years earlier and saved $100 every year. Michelle waited until she was 39 and even though she saved twice as much - $200 every year – she saved about $2,000 less than Jonathon. It's hard to believe, isn't it? If you still have trouble believing us, go online to a compound interest calculator and play around with some numbers. Here's one place to start: www.bankrate.com.

Step #8: Wrap it Up

Get yourselves something to write with and share your answers to the following questions.

Question	Adult	Teenager
Are you saving now?		
Does your saving-investing plan include regular deposits? (Weekly or monthly?)		
What interest rate are you earning on your savings?		
Is there a higher interest rate offered through a CD or money-market account? What is it? (Go to your bank and ask or go online and check.)		
Research one other bank or credit union. What interest rates on savings does it offer?		
Are you curious about the stock market? How much money can you devote to investing in a stock or two?		

Have your teenager begin saving and investing NOW and they will be on their way to having options and financial independence. Don't wait!

Step #9: *It's Not Just For Rich People: Personal Net Worth*

Your teenager lives in a highly materialistic society. In fact, we all do. But teenagers usually don't understand that most of the materialism they see is not a measure of wealth. The fancy cars, mansionized homes, and designer clothing that many of their friends, acquaintances, and strangers flaunt are bought using credit. And often the people who lead understated lives are the ones who have built real wealth and have many more options. A final thought that we recommend you share with your teenager is about personal net worth.

Net worth is a simple calculation: assets minus liabilities. Have your teenager add up all the things they 'own' - their possessions worth over $100, bank accounts, any investments, car, etc. These are their **assets**. Have them write down that number in the table below. Next, have them add up all the debts that they owe; credit card balances, any loans they have. These are their **liabilities**. Have them write down that number. Now subtract and write the answer next to 'Net Worth'.

Explain to them that if they lost their job (if they have one) and had to sell everything they owned of value and used that money to pay off their debts, the money left over (net worth) is what they'd have to live on. Ask them, "How long could you survive on that money without a job?" Most teenagers we know could survive between one day to one month. Ask them if they are horrified by their answer, concerned but not panicked, or comfortable. People who have built real wealth and are truly 'rich' know that if they lost their job, they have assets worth real money that they can count on for a long period of time – a year or more. Then ask them what they think their net worth should be in order to be 'rich', valued in number of months or years. It's at this point in the lesson that our students often say, "Jeez, I need to have a whole bunch of money if I'm going to be truly rich!"

CALCULATING NET WORTH

Assets	
Liabilities	
Net Worth	

We strongly recommend that you have your teenager read the following story. We think it says it all about net worth and life options and it came right out of the classroom.

DOLLARS & $ENSE

Anna strutted into class like she owned the building. Starbucks drink in hand, texting on her iPhone, BMW keys dangling from her pinkie finger. She was so proud the car, which her parents had given to her for her 18th, she continually advertised it. She slung herself and her Burberry jacket and French tipped nails into a desk chair looking as if she's doing us all a favor.

A few minutes later, in shuffled Matt – baggy jeans, boxy t-shirt, generic boy uniform. Behind a grimy curtain of hair, he checked his cell phone – low-end, unidentifiable model – and hid somewhere in the back row, as the class filled in.

Today's lesson was about personal net worth. Net worth isn't something only Bill Gates gets to have. We all do. And it's important if you want to take out a loan or start a new business because it determines how much money you might be able to borrow and at what cost. In the world of personal finance, net worth is determined by adding up all of the things you own of value (assets) and then adding together all of the debts you owe (liabilities). Now subtract. The resulting number is your net worth. After some discussion about examples of assets and liabilities, the students calculated their personal net worth.

Volunteers began to share their net worth with the class. "Twenty bucks, fully clothed," said one. "Zero dollahs, I travel light," said another. And: "Maybe like $1,000 if I sold my computer and iPod, but then, why live!"

Then someone blurted out, "Hey Anna, what's yours?" Anna looked sickened and confused. She kept staring at the calculation she made on her paper and finally said in a faint voice, "it's really low." Another student asked, "What about that Beemer, isn't that worth like $70,000?"

Anna's friend quickly answered, "Yeah, but it's leased, she doesn't own it."

Out of the corner of my eye, I saw Matt's hand in the air. When I called on him, he offered his own number: $150,000. All heads swiveled and eyes bulged. Another student asked, "How'd you get that number?"

"My family bought a small walnut farm a long time ago and now that I'm 18 it's legally mine," Matt said. "Oh yeah, and there's no debt on it".

For about 10 seconds there was total silence. "Damn, Matt, you could actually pay for college or start your own business if you sold that land," someone finally said.

In those few precious moments, without designer anything, without a car, without hip techno-gadgets, Matt had taught his peers one of the most important lessons about money – Matt had options.

A Final Word From Your Authors

As high school teachers of finance we want every student to have options – to not live paycheck to paycheck throughout their lives. By exposing your teenager to the fundamentals of personal finance, you will find that not only do they become empowered to make financial-related decisions, but they begin to make **better** financial-related decisions. Congratulations! You have given your child some of the tools for financial success. Some day, they may say "thank you!"

Chapter Ten Checklist:

Check off the items you and your teenager have completed:

- ☐ 1. Discuss basic savings terms.
- ☐ 2. Discuss the concept of compound interest and the compounding effect of money.
- ☐ 3. Discuss basic investments and share personal investment history.
- ☐ 4. Explore at least one investment opportunity.
- ☐ 5. Open an IRA (when child is 18).
- ☐ 6. Meet with a financial advisor.
- ☐ 7. Have teenager calculate their net worth.

Useful Websites:

- Investopedia.com
- Younginvestor.com
- Virtualstockexchange.com
- Bankrate.com
- Youngmoney.com
- Finance.yahoo.com
- Irs.gov

Notes

About the Authors

Alyson Amy Edge (left) and Patricia Saunders Garfield (right) are high school teachers and parents. Together they have been working with teenagers and their parents for 29 years.

Alyson has been teaching accounting and other business related courses for 19 years. She currently serves as the director of the Academy of Finance at Burbank High School, a chapter of the National Academy Foundation. She was the Burbank Unified School District Teacher of the Year in 2004. In addition to her teaching credential from California State University Northridge, Alyson holds a BA in General Studies and a minor in Business Administration from Northern Arizona University. Alyson lives in Burbank, California with her husband and stepson.

Patricia has been teaching personal finance, economics and other business-related courses for 10 years. Prior to teaching, Patricia began her career in corporate business where she spent 15 years in sales, marketing and strategic planning. In addition to her California State teaching credential, Patricia holds a BS in Business Administration from the University of Colorado and a MBA from Pepperdine University. Patricia lives in La Canada, California with her husband and two children.

Glossary

accreditation – A process whereby a school, college, university or technical educational institute is given a certification of competency, authority, or credibility.

APR – Annual percentage rate. The cost of credit expressed as a yearly percentage.

APY – Annual percentage yield. The actual interest rate an account pays per year with compounding included.

assets – Items of value that a person owns.

automatic payroll deductions – Diversions of income from gross pay by an employer to help facilitate saving, investment, and other pre-tax deductions for the employee.

bank or commercial bank – An institution for receiving, keeping, and lending money.

bond – A debt obligation of corporations or federal, state or local governments. Usually paid back over time with interest.

bounced check – When an overdraft occurs and a check is returned.

brokerage firm – A financial institution that facilitates the buying and selling of investments such as stocks, bonds, mutual funds and other financially-related products.

budget – A sum of money set aside each month to pay for specific expenses.

capital gain – An increase in the value of stock above the price initially paid.

capitalized cost (as in a car lease) – The price for a leased car. Also known as the lease price.

car lease – A written agreement that allows a person to use an automobile for a specified time period and payment.

cash advance fee – A fixed amount charged when a credit card is used to obtain cash.

cash flow – The inflows (income) and outflows (expenses) of money through a household or business.

certificate of deposit or CD – A deposit made by an individual to a bank or credit union that earns a fixed interest rate for a specified length of time.

charitable organization - A type of non-profit organization centered around goals of a general philanthropic nature (e.g. charitable, educational, religious, or other activities serving the public interest or common good).

check – A written order instructing a bank to pay a stated amount to a person or business named on the order by deducting an equivalent amount from the check writer's checking account.

checking account – An account offered by banks and credit unions that allows an account holder to deposit funds, withdraw funds, check current balances, perform online banking, and write checks.

checking account register or checkbook register – A booklet used to record checking account transactions.

collision coverage – Automobile insurance that protects your own car against damage from accidents or vehicle overturning.

compounding effect of money – Money invested that yields a positive rate of return.

compound interest – Interest that applies to both the principal and the interest of a loan.

comprehensive coverage – Insurance that pays for damage to your car from events other than collision or vehicle overturning.

co-signer – A person who promises in writing to repay a financial obligation if the original debtor fail to pay.

cover letter – A letter of introduction accompanying a resume. The cover letter explains a job applicant's suitability for a desired position.

credit bureau – A company that gathers, stores, and sells credit information to business subscribers.

credit card – A plastic card that represents a loan from a bank or credit union to purchase things now with the ability to pay back the borrowed money later.

credit card balance – What is owed to the bank, credit union or credit card company for the charges accumulated from using a credit card.

credit card statement – An accounting by the credit card issuer of all charges and fees associated with a credit card. It may be viewed online or received monthly by mail.

credit history – A complete record of a person's borrowing and repayment performance over time.

credit report – A written statement of a consumer's credit history, issued by a credit bureau to its business subscribers.

credit score – A numerical expression (a number) based on a statistical analysis of a person's credit history, representing the likelihood of the person's ability to repay debt.

credit limit – The amount the credit-card issuer is willing to loan a credit-cardholder.

credit union – Not-for-profit organization established by groups of employees in similar occupations who pool their money. It offers many services similar to that of a bank.

debit card – A plastic card that allows immediate deductions from a checking account to pay for purchases.

deductions – 1. Amounts subtracted from gross pay to arrive at take home pay or net pay. 2. Amounts subtracted from gross pay on a tax return.

depreciated amount (as in a car lease) – The

amount of a car you 'use up' while driving, expressed as a percentage or dollar figure.

diversification – The spreading of risk among many types of investments.

dividend – A portion of a corporation's profits paid to its stockholder.

down payment – A part of the purchase price paid in cash up front, reducing the amount of the loan or lease.

FAFSA or Free Application for Federal Student Aid – An application to determine if a college student is eligible for a Federal financial aid.

federal income tax – A tax levied by Congress on the income of individuals and businesses.

federal work-study program or work study – A financial aid program that allows a student to work part-time while going to school to pay for some of their education.

finance charges – Fees applied for services or as penalties associated with credit cards.

financial advisor – A trained financial planner who gives overall investment advice based on your goals, age, lifestyle, and other factors.

fixed expense – A financial cost required to be pay at specific times, regardless of other events.

Form W2 – A form that lists income earned during the year and all amounts withheld by the employer for taxes.

Form W4 – A form completed for income tax withholding purposes.

grant – Student financial aid that doesn't require repayment.

gross pay – The amount of income earned before any deductions are subtracted.

hourly wage – An amount earned for each hour worked.

Individual Retirement Account (IRA) – A retirement savings plan that allows individuals to set aside money in tax-deferred savings up to a limit set by the government.

informational interview – An interview to gain information about a job, career, industry or company. It is not a job interview.

insurance – A method for spreading individual risk among a large group of people to make losses more affordable for all.

insurer – A business (usually an insurance company) that agrees to pay the cost of potential future losses in exchange for regular fee payments.

interest – 1. Money paid for the use of money. 2. Earnings on certain investments.

interest charges - The APR (percent) applied to any credit card balance that is not paid in full by the due date.

interest rate – 1. The cost of borrowing money expressed as a percent. 2. A sum of money received for lending, saving, or investing money expressed as a percent.

Internal Revenue Service or IRS – The federal government agency that collects taxes.

internship – Any period of time during which a beginner acquires experience in an occupation, profession, or pursuit. It may be paid or unpaid.

investing – The use of savings to earn a financial return.

job shadowing – Following a worker as he or she performs a job with the intention of learning more about a particular line of work.

late fee – A fixed amount charged for a late payment.

liabilities – Amounts of money owed to others.

liability coverage – Insurance to protect against claims for bodily injury to another person or damage to another person's property.

loan – A sum of money given today with the agreement that the sum will be repaid in the future.

maturity (of an investment) – The date on which an investment is repaid.

Medicare taxes – Taxes that provide hospital and medical insurance for elderly retired individuals and for some disabled individuals.

money factor – A numerical value expressed as a decimal that when multiplied by 2400 is equivalent to the annual percentage rate used in a car lease. Also known as the lease rate.

money-market account – A combination savings-investment plan in which money deposited is used to purchase safe, liquid securities.

MSRP (manufacturer's suggested retail price) – The recommended amount a manufacturer tells a retailer to price a car for sale.

mutual fund – A large, professionally managed group of investments.

net pay or take home pay – The amount left after all deductions have been taken out of your gross pay.

net worth – The difference between assets and liabilities.

no-fault insurance – Automobile insurance that reimburses the medical costs and repair expenses of a driver under that driver's own policy without seeking reimbursement from the person who may have caused the accident.

on-line banking - A bank or credit union service that allows an account holder to pay bills or transfer funds from a computer or cell phone.

overdraft – A check written for more money than your checking account contains.

overdraft fees – Fees that are charged by a bank or credit union for an overdraft.

overdraft protection – A service provided by a bank or credit union that allow checks and withdrawals to be made even when there are insufficient funds in the checking account. Fees will be charged for this protection.

over-the-limit-fee – A fixed amount charged when the credit-cardholder charges more than their credit limit.

overtime – The time worked beyond the regular hours; usually more than 40 hours in a five-day period. Often times paid at a higher rate than regular hourly pay; known as overtime pay.

personal injury protection (PIP) – Automobile insurance that pays for medical, hospital, and funeral costs of the insured and his or her family and passengers, regardless of fault.

policy – A written insurance contract.

policyholder – The person who owns an insurance policy.

poverty threshold or poverty line – The amount of income that determines government benefits such as food stamps and welfare payments.

premium – The fee a policyholder agrees to pay to an insurance company periodically (monthly, quarterly, annually, or semiannually) for an insurance policy.

principal – 1. The amount borrowed, or the unpaid portion of the amount borrowed, on which the borrower pays interest; as in the case of a credit card and a loan. 2. The amount of money deposited by a saver; as in the case of a savings account or investment vehicle.

progressive tax – A tax that takes a larger share of income as the amount of income grows. The U.S. Federal income tax is a progressive tax.

rate of return – The ratio of money gained or lost on an investment relative to the amount of money invested, expressed as a percent.

reference page – A written document listing contact information for individuals who will attest to skills and abilities of a job applicant.

residual value (as in a car lease) – The wholesale value of a car at the end of a lease.

resume – A written summary of work experience, education, abilities, interests, and other information that may be of interest to an employer.

room and board – A situation where, in exchange for money, labor or other considerations, a person is provided with a place to live as well as meals on a comprehensive basis. Often referring to a living situation on college campuses.

Rule of 72 – Technique for estimating the number of years required to double your money at a given rate of return.

salary – An annual amount earned for full-time employment regardless of any extra time worked over and beyond scheduled hours.

SAR or Student Aid Report – A report that contains the information reported on a FAFSA and contains the Expected Family Contribution. Schools listed on a FAFSA will get the SAR data electronically and will use it to determine how much federal student aid the school is offering.

savings account - An account at a bank that pays interest on the deposits within the account.

scholarship – A sum of money or other aid granted to a student for a variety of reasons. Repayment is not required.

security deposit – A refundable amount paid in advance to protect the owner against damage or non-payment. Security deposits are often required when leasing a car, an apartment or home.

Social Security taxes – Taxes that provide federal aid (money) for the elderly and for disabled individuals.

standard of living – Standard of living refers to the level of wealth, comfort, material goods and necessities available to a certain socioeconomic class in a certain geographic area

state income tax – A tax levied by a state legislature on the income of individuals and businesses.

stock – A unit of ownership in a corporation.

stockholder or shareholder – An owner of a corporation.

stock market – A physical or virtual place where buyers and sellers of stock come together for the purpose of exchange.

student loan – A contract between a student and the lender; usually a bank or the government. The lender agrees to lend the student money for tuition and other costs and the student agrees to pay the money back over time with interest.

tax – A financial charge imposed by a government on income, products, and services.

tax deduction – A reduction of income subject to tax.

tax evasion – Willful failure to pay taxes.

taxable income – The income on which you pay tax.

tax return – A form, required by the IRS, that reflects all the income earned, taxes paid, and other specific information on financial transactions. (Forms 1040EZ and 1040 are two tax return forms mentioned in Chapter 9.)

term (of an investment) – The length of time associated with a specific investment.

title – A legal document that establishes ownership.

tuition – Fees paid to colleges for instruction and other educational expenses.

uninsured/underinsured motorist coverage – Automobile insurance that pays for your injuries when the other driver is legally liable but unable to pay.

variable expense – Costs that vary in amount and type, depending on events and the choices made.

Index

Made in the USA
San Bernardino, CA
21 September 2014